STUDIES IN INDIAN ANTIQUITIES

STUDIES IN INDIAN ANTIQUITIES

BY

HEMCHANDRA RAYCHAUDHURI

GYAN

Published by

Gyan Publishing House
5, Ansari Road
Daryaganj, New Delhi-110002
Phone: 011-47034999, 9811692060
E-mail: books@gyanbooks.com

Distribution Network
gyanbooks.com
India, USA, Canada, UK, Australia

ISBN: 978-93-6280-250-7 (PB)
First Published, 1932

2nd Impression 2024

Printed at: Gyan Press, Delhi.

STUDIES IN INDIAN ANTIQUITIES
Author: HEMCHANDRA RAYCHAUDHURI

STUDIES IN INDIAN ANTIQUITIES

STUDIES IN INDIAN ANTIOUITIES

BY

HEMCHANDRA RAYCHAUDHURI, M.A., PH.D.

LECTURER IN HISTORY, CALCUTTA UNIVERSITY ; FORMERLY PROFESSOR OF HISTORY, PRESIDENCY COLLEGE, CALCUTTA AND READER AND ACTING HEAD OF THE DEPARTMENT OF HISTORY, DACCA UNIVERSITY ; AUTHOR OF 'POLITICAL HISTORY OF ANCIENT INDIA,' 'EARLY HISTORY OF THE VAISHNAVA SECT,' ETC., ETC.

PUBLISHED BY THE

UNIVERSITY OF CALCUTTA

1932

भुवनेशीं नमस्कृत्य वाग्देवीं वर्णमातृकाम् ।
मातरं पितरञ्चैव कीर्त्तयिष्यामि भारतम् ॥

PREFACE

This little volume is, in the main, a collection of detached essays, which is intended to serve as an introduction to the study of some vexed problems of Indian antiquity, particularly of the early epic and the geographical sections of the *Purāṇas*. The papers now collected appeared at different times in various literary and historical journals, monthly reviews, vernacular magazines, commemoration volumes, and miscellaneous compilations such as *the Calcutta Review, the Journal of the Department of Letters, the Journal of the Asiatic Society of Bengal, the Indian Antiquary, the Indian Historical Quarterly, the Navya-Bhārata, the Mānasī o Marmavāṇi, the Vichitrā, Sir Asutosh Mookerjee Silver Jubilee Volumes,* and Law's *Buddhistic Studies*. To the editors and publishers of these works the writer of the following pages takes this opportunity of offering his sincere thanks. The re-issue of the articles has afforded him an opportunity of correcting some typographical mistakes, or other errors, that crept into the texts as published in the periodicals and miscellanies named above, particularly the Bengali magazines. Ancient Indian History is a progressive subject, and it is not surprising that, while subjecting the papers to revision, additions, emendations and re-arrangements have, in some cases, been deemed to be necessary.

The essays, disquisitions and notes brought together in the present volume are grouped under four heads, *viz.* (I) Vedic and Epic Studies, (II) Geography, (III) History and Chronology and (IV) Epic and Geographical Studies in Bengali. While the book as a whole undoubtedly suffers from a lack of unity, Part II, *viz.*, that dealing with Ancient Indian Geography, will, it is hoped, be found to be comparatively free from the defects inherent in an assemblage of independent treatises.

The papers constituting Part I relate to the Vedas and the Epics. The dissertations on the epics have already been noticed by scholars like Washburn Hopkins (*Ethics of India*, p. 171 n) and M. Winternitz (*A History of Indian Literature*, Vol. I, translated from the original German by Mrs. S. Ketkar and revised by the author, pp. 473 n, 506 n), while that on *the Antiquity of the Ṛigveda* has been commented on by Professor A. B. Keith in *the Religion and Philosophy of the Veda and Upanishads*, p. 618. The Professor's remark that the writer of the paper based his conclusions only on "the epic or Purāṇa genealogies" is perhaps due to an oversight, as the author referred not only to the *Rāja-paramparā* of the epics and the *Purāṇas*, but also to the *Āchārya-paramparā* of the Vedic texts, particularly of the *Śatapatha*

Brāhmaṇa and the *Śāṅkhāyana Āraṇyaka*. The essayist was certainly not unaware of the fact that "the *Mahābhārata*, in its present shape, is a late work" and that "the tradition recorded in the *Ādi-parva*" was regarded by some scholars as "mere folklore, useless for historical purposes." He, therefore, adduced evidence from the Vedic texts and observed that "The agreement between the *Brāhmaṇas*, the *Upanishads*, and the epic, and the synchronisms established, confirm and corroborate one another and tend to show that the *Rāja-paramparā* and the *Guru-paramparā* are entitled to credence."

The writer of the following pages craves the indulgence of the reader for any mistake and misprint that may have escaped his attention. He owes a special debt of gratitude to Mr. J. C. Chakravorti, Asistant Registrar, Calcutta University, who lent his aid at various stages of the work. His thanks are also due to Mr. A. C. Ghatak, the Superintendent of the University Press, and his Assistants, for help in reading the proofs.

THE UNIVERSITY OF CALCUTTA : H. C. R. C.
June 14, 1932.

LIST OF ABBREVIATIONS.

Afif.	...	Shams-i-Sirāj 'Afîf.
A. G. I.	...	Ancient Geography of India (Cunningham).
Araṇya.	...	Araṇya-Kāṇḍa of the Rāmāyaṇa.
Arch. S. R. / A. S. R.	...	Reports of the Archaeological Survey of India.
A. S. I.	...	Archaeological Survey of India (Annual Reports).
Bhāg. P.	...	Bhāgavata Purāṇa.
Bomb. Gaz.	...	Bombay Gazetteer.
Bṛih. Up.	...	Bṛhadāraṇyaka Upanishad.
Cal. Rev.	...	Calcutta Review.
Camb. Hist. Ind.	...	The Cambridge History of India, Vol. I.
C. I. I. / Corpus.	...	Corpus Inscriptionum Indicarum.
C. P.	...	The Central Provinces.
Cunn.	...	Cunningham.
Dist. Gaz.	...	District Gazetteer.
E. H. I.[4]	...	Early History of India (V. A. Smith), 4th edition.
Ep. Ind.	...	Epigraphia Indica.
H. S.	...	Harsha Samvat (Era).
Imp. Gaz.	...	Imperial Gazetteer.

I. A. / Ind. Ant.	Indian Antiquary.
Ind. Lit.	Indian Literature.
Ins.	Inscription.
Jaiminiya Up. Br.	Jaiminîya Upanishad Brāhmaṇa.
JASB.	Journal of the Asiatic Society of Bengal.
JBORS.	Journal of the Bihār and Orissa Research Society.
J & P ASB (N.S.)	Journal and Proceedings of the Asiatic Society of Bengal (New Series).
JRAS.	Journal of the Royal Asiatic Society.
Kaush. Up.	Kaushîtaki Upanishad.
Kish.	Kishkindhyā-Kāṇḍa of the Rāmāyaṇa.
Lank.	Lankā-kāṇḍa of the Rāmāyaṇa.
Mārk. P.	Mārkaṇḍeya Purāṇa.
Mbh.	Mahābhārata.
Mem. ASB.	Memoir of the Asiatic Society of Bengal.
Pro.	Proceedings.
Raghu.	Raghu-vaṁśa (Kālidāsa).
Rām.	Rāmāyaṇa.
Rig. V. / R. V.	Ṛig Veda.
Sans. Lit.	Sanskrit Literature.

Sat. Br.	...	Śatapatha Brāhmaṇa.
T. S.	...	Taittirîya Saṁhitā.
U. P.	...	The United Provinces.
Uttara.	...	Uttara-Kāṇḍa of the Rāmāyaṇa.
Vastr.	...	Vastrāpatha-māhātmya of the Skanda Purāṇa.
Ved. Ind.	...	Vedic Index.
V. S.	...	Vikrama Saṁvat.
W. S. W.	...	West South West.
Z.D.M.G.	...	Zeitschrift der Deutschen Morgenländischen Gesellschaft.

CONTENTS

Part I

Vedic and Epic Studies

Part II

Geography

Part III

History and Chronology

Part IV

Epic and Geographical Studies (in Bengali)

PART I

VEDIC AND EPIC STUDIES

STUDIES IN INDIAN ANTIQUITIES

PART I

Vedic and Epic Studies

CHAPTER I

The Antiquity of the Rig Veda

The date of the *Ṛig Veda* has been the subject of much discussion and controversy Scholars are not wanting who would place it in the Miocene or the Pliocene epoch, while others would bring it down to the close of the second, or the beginning of the first, millennium B.C. There is, however, a consensus of opinion regarding its comparative antiquity, and it is almost universally accepted that the *Ṛig Veda* is older than the rest of Indian Literature, and that even the latest parts of the work are much older than Buddha Śākyamuni. But the number of centuries which separated the latest hymns from the time of the founder of Buddhism is a matter regarding which there is the widest divergence of opinion.

Max Müller, starting from the date of Alexander's invasion, and assigning a period of two hundred years for the development of each of the four literary strata discernible in the Vedic Literature, arrived at the date 1200 to 1000 B.C. as the beginning of Vedic poetry, and his view has been accepted by scholars like Macdonell and Keith. Tilak and Jacobi, on the other hand, tried to push the date much farther back on astronomical grounds. But, as pointed out by Macdonell,[1] Keith[2] and Winternitz[3] it is not safe to build a chronological edifice on a foundation the solidity of which is subject to grave doubts. The last-mentioned scholar justly attaches greater importance to historical and geographical arguments, and it is to such arguments that we shall adhere in this humble treatise.

Professor Winternitz seeks to show that the *Ṛig Veda* is the oldest literary work in India. While accepting the general observations of the Professor regarding the priority of the *Ṛig Veda* to the other Vedic texts, and to the earliest literature of the Jains and the Buddhists, we confess that we find it difficult to follow some of his arguments, particularly those which lead him to think that the age of the *Ṛig Veda* must be placed nearer the date assumed by Jacobi and Tilak than to that adopted by Max Müller.

[1] Sans. Lit., p. 12.

[2] Camb. Hist., pp. 111-112.

[3] Cal. Rev., Nov. 1923, p. 126.

Thus it is impossible to endorse the view that "during the whole time from the first beginnings to the last off-shoots of Vedic literature the Indo-Aryan people have only conquered the comparatively small area from the Indus to the Ganges." The *Aitareya Brāhmaṇa* is certainly older than the "last off-shoots of Vedic literature," and in it we have a reference to several kingdoms of *Dakshiṇā Diś* or the Southern Region, and in particular to the Aryan kingdom of Vidarbha (Berar) whose king Bhîma received instruction regarding the substitute for the Soma juice through a succession of teachers from Parvata and Nārada. King Bhîma was only fourth in spiritual succession from Somaka, son of Sahadeva, who is mentioned in the *Ṛig Veda* (iv. 15. 7-8). The *Bṛihadāraṇyaka Upanishad* mentions a teacher named Vidarbhî Kauṇḍinya whose name marks him out as an inhabitant of the city of Kuṇḍina in Vidarbha, and who was only three generations removed from Ayāsya Aṅgirasa or Āṅgirasa, a *Ṛig Vedic ṛishi*, the composer of many *Ṛig Vedic* hymns.[1] The *Śatapatha Brāhmaṇa* refers to Naḍa Naishadha, a southern king, whose realm Nishadha lay in the Vindhyan region.[2]

[1] *Cf.* x. 67. 1; 108. 8; ix. 44-46; x. 67; 68; Ved. Ind., i. 32; Bṛih. Up., ii. 6; iv. 6.

[2] Sat.Br., ii. 2, 2, 1. 2; Mārk. Purāṇa, lvii. 54-55.

It is thus clear that not only the Ganges valley, but a considerable portion of Central India and the Deccan was Aryanised long before "the last off-shoots of Vedic Literature." Consequently we fail to appreciate the force of the following arguments of Winternitz, "if it took such a long time for Aryan Civilisation to spread only from the extreme north-west to the eastern Ganges district, how many centuries must have been required not only for Vedic literature but at the same time also for Brāhmaṇical culture, theology and even priestly supremacy to pervade the whole of Central and Southern India." Let us not be misunderstood; the Aryanisation of India was certainly not accomplished in a day. But Winternitz's estimate of the requisite period is, in our opinion, based on a wrong premise.

Again when Winternitz says that the *Ṛig Veda* is older than Pārśva he is probably correct, but in the absence of genuine works which can, with any amount of certainty, be referred to Pārśva himself, can it be said with confidence that the *Veda* must have been completed and considered as the sacred text of Brāhmaṇism as early as the eighth century B. C. (the age of Pārśva)? The truth is that although Winternitz is right in holding that the *Ṛig Veda* is more ancient than any other literary product of India, yet when he actually tries to measure the distance which separates the work from well-known chronological epochs his arguments are not quite convincing.

But are there no hints and indications in the Vedic literature itself which may help us to arrive at an approximate date of the *Ṛik Saṁhitā?* We think there are, and it will be our endeavour in this treatise to draw the attention of scholars to a few facts which, while they do not solve the problem, lend some additional weight to the brilliant conjecture of Max Müller.

In the 98th Sūkta of the 10th Mandala of the *Rik Saṁhitā* mention is made of two personages named Śaṁtanu and Devāpi whom Yāska represents as two brothers, sons of a Kuru king. The younger Śaṁtanu became king, Devāpi having made choice of a life of penance. It is impossible not to recognise in these two scions of the Kuru royal family, the famous Kuru king Śaṁtanu and his ascetic brother Devāpi immortalised in the pages of the *Mahābhārata.*[1] According to the Great Epic king

The epithet Ārshṭishena applied to Devāpi does not necessarily indicate that he was the *son* of Ṛishṭishena, any more than the epithet Gairikshita applied to Paurukutsya, *i.e.*, Trasadasyu (Ṛig V., 33. 8), shows that he was the son of Girikshit, or the epithet Saudyumni applied to Bharata Dauḥṣanti shows that he was the son of Sudyumna. Ṛishṭishena may have been a remote ancestor of Devāpi, or the name might have been a secondary epithet of Pratīpa, as Vasushena of Karṇa and Mahāsena of Pradyota. As to the epithet Aulāna which, according to

Śaṁtanu was sixth in the ascending line from Parikshit (son of Abhimanyu who died in the Bhārata War). If this tradition has any value the end of the *Ṛig Vedic* period cannot be separated by more than six generations from the time of the last mentioned sovereign. It may, however, be argued that the *Mahābhārata*, in its present shape, is a late work, and the tradition recorded in the *Ādi-parva* regarding the relationship between Śaṁtanu and Parikshit is mere folklore, useless for historical purposes. But the main conclusion at which we have arrived, namely, that the *Ṛig Veda* is separated by not more than six generations from the time of Parikshit, receives striking confirmation from another quarter. We have already referred to the sage Ayāsya Āṅgirasa who is the composer of many of the hymns of the *Ṛig Veda*, and who is mentioned by name in the tenth *Maṇḍala*. In two lists of teachers given in the *Bṛihadāraṇyaka Upanishad* (ii.6; iv.6) this sage is represented as being ninth in the ascending line from Vātsya, pupil of Śāṇḍilya, whereas Tura Kāvasheya, the priest of Parikshit's son(and Abhimanyu's grandson),[1] is only fifth in the

some, refers to Śaṁtanu it may be pointed outt hat 'Ilina is actually mentioned in the dynastic lists of the Mahābhārata as the name of an ancestor of Śaṁtanu. The name had variants, and the real name may have been Ulana as the Ṛigvedic word suggests.

1 *Bhāgavata Purāṇa*, ix. 22, 25-26; *Aitareya Brāhmaṇa*, viii. 21.

ascending line from the same teacher (Vātsya) as we learn from the *Śatapatha Brāhmaṇa* (end of Book X). In other words, Ayāsya is separated by four or five generations from Tura as will appear from the following table :—

Ayāsya Āṅgirasa	...	
Pathin Saubhara	...	
Vatsanapāt Bābhrava	...	
Vidarbhî Kauṇḍinya	...	
Gālava	...	Tura Kāvasheya.
Kumāra Hārita	...	Yajñavachas Rājastambāyana.
Kaiśorya Kāpya	...	Kuśri.
Śāṇḍilya	...	Śāṇḍilya.
Vātsya	...	Vātsya.

We are further told by the *Bṛihadāraṇyaka Upanishad* that Ayāsya flourished thirteen or fourteen generations before Āsuri (a near spiritual ancestor of Āsurāyaṇa), while a perusal of page 18 of the *Political History of Ancient India from the Accession of Parikshit to the Coronation of Bimbiśāra* (first edition) will show that Tura Kāvasheya was only seven generations removed from the same teacher (Āsuri). According to this calculation Ayāsya was six or seven generations removed from Tura. It is clear that Ayāsya was older by not less than four, nor more than six or seven generations from the time of Tura Kāvasheya and his contemporary Janamejaya, son of Parikshit. We must make allowance for the difference of one or two generations while comparing the various lists of teachers, because all the *Ṛishis* did not live for an equal length of time. Moreover, we have instances in which a teacher appears both as *Guru* and *Parama Guru* of the same person. We may take six as the mean number of generations which separated the teachers Ayāsya and Tura.[1] If the *Mahābhārata* tradition

[1] The conclusion at which we have arrived from a study of the *Āchārya-paramparā* in the *Bṛihadāraṇyaka Upanishad* is strikingly confirmed by the *Sāṅkhāyana Āraṇyaka*. That work gives a list of teachers according to which Viśvāmitra and Devarāta (Śunaḥ-śepa), the composers of many Ṛigvedic hymns, who, according to the *Aitareya Brāhmaṇa*, are contemporaries of Ayāsya Āṅgirasa, are 15th and 14th respectively in the ascending line from Guṇākhya Śāṅkhāyana, whereas Tura Kāvasheya, the priest of Janamejaya Pārikshita, is only eighth in the ascending line from the same teacher (*Political History of Ancient India*, first edition, pp. 9, 18).

1. Viśvāmitra	...	...
2. Devarāta	...	...
3. Sākamaśva	...	...
4. Vyaśva	...	...
5. Viśvamanā	...	...
6. Uddālaka	...	...
7. Sumnayu	...	...
8. Bṛihaddiva	...	8. Tura Kāvasheya.
9. Prativeśya	...	9. Yajñavachas Rājastambāyana.

regarding the relationship between Saṁtanu and Parikshit has any value this would make Ayāsya a contemporary of Saṁtanu, and an elder contemporary of the Ṛishi Parāśara who is well-known in the Epic as a contemporary of the second wife of that king. That our surmise is probably correct is proved by the evidence of the *Aitareya* and *Sāmavidhāna Brāhmaṇas*. According to the story of Sunaḥ-śepa narrated in the *Aitareya* (vii. 13-18)—which in the opinion of Winternitz himself is a legend of time-honoured age—Ayāsya was the *Udgātā* of king Hariśchandra whose court was visited by Parvata and Nārada. Consequently Ayāsya and Nārada were contemporaries. Now the *Sāmavidhāna Brāhmaṇa*[1] tells us that Nārada taught Vishvaksena and the latter taught Vyāsa Pārāśarya (son of Parāśara). Parāśara, father of Vyāsa, was thus, on the evidence of the *Brāhmaṇa*, a contemporary of Vishvaksena and a junior contemporary of Nārada and of Ayāsya if, as is possible, Nārada of the *Sām vidhāna*

10. Sauma Prātiveśya ...	10. Kuśri.
11. Somapa	11. Śāṇḍilya.
12. Priyavrata Saumāpi ...	12. Vātsya.
13. Uddālaka Āruṇi ...	13. Vāmakakshāyaṇa ; Uddālaka Āruṇi.
14. Kahola Kaushitaki ...	14. Yājñavalkya and Kahola.
15. Guṇākhya Śāṅkhāyana	15. Guṇākhya Śāṅkhāyana.

1 Ved. Ind., ii, pp. 315, 339.

Brāhmaṇa be identical with his namesake of the *Aitareya*. And this is just the conclusion at which we have arrived from a study of the *Bṛihadāraṇyaka Upanishad* and the *Mahābhārata.* The agreement between the *Brāhmaṇas*, the *Upanishad* and the *Epic*, and the synchronisms established, confirm and corroborate one another and tend to show that the *Rāja-paramparā* and the *Guru-paramparā* to which we have drawn attention, are entitled to credence. We have no valid reason, therefore, for doubting their authenticity and historical value. If that be so, it is impossible to believe that Śaṁtanu and Ayāsya could be more than six or seven generations older than Janamejaya Pārikshita and Tura Kāvasheya. Now Rhys Davids in his Buddhist Suttas adduces good grounds for assigning a period of hundred and fifty years to the five Theras from Upāli to Mahinda. If the five Theras be assigned a period of hundred and fifty years, the six or seven teachers from Ayāsya to Tura may be assigned a period of two centuries. And the tenth *Maṇḍala* of the *Ṛig Veda* referring to Ayāsya could not have been composed more than two hundred years before the time of Janamejaya, the patron of Tura. In the *Political History of Ancient India* we have tried to show that Parikshit, father of Janamejaya, flourished probably in the 9th century B.C. In that case the date of the hymns mentioning Ayāsya cannot be earlier than the 11th century B.C. Even if we accept the Purāṇic date (1,015 years before Nanda, *i.e.*, 14th century B.C.) for Parikshit, father of Janamejaya, the *Ṛig Veda* could not have been completed earlier than the 16th century B. C.

It may be argued that the tenth *Maṇḍala* of the *Ṛik Saṁhitā* is a later addition. Is there any evidence that some of the other *Maṇḍalas* were known at the time of Ayāsya and Śaṁtanu? Fortunately the *Aitareya Brāhmaṇa* throws a flood of light on the solution of this question also. In the Śunaḥ-śepa legend Ayāsya is mentioned as a contemporary not only of Nārada but also of Vasishṭha, of Viśvāmitra father of Madhuchchhandas, of Madhuchchhandas himself and of Śunaḥ-śepa, adopted son of Viśvāmitra. Now Viśvāmitra, *sunu* (son) of Kuśika (*i.e.*, father of Madhuchchhandas), is mentioned as the author of several hymns of the third *Maṇḍala*, while his son Madhuchchhandas is the *ṛishi* of the very first hymns of the first and ninth *Maṇḍalas*. Śunaḥ-śepa is mentioned in the *Ṛig Veda*, i. 24. 13 and v. 2. 7. The seventh book refers to Vasishṭha, grandfather of Parāśara and contemporary of Viśvāmitra, *sunu* of Kuśika, and what is more important, it mentions Parāśara himself who, as we have seen, was a younger contemporary of Ayāsya and is, moreover, the *Ṛishi* of the hymns, i. 65 *et seq*. If the evidence of the *Aitareya Brāhmaṇa* has any value, part of the first, third, fifth, seventh and ninth Maṇḍalas of the *Ṛig Veda* will have to be dated in or about the time of Ayāsya.[1] Thus a large part, if not the whole, of the *Ṛik Saṁhitā* was composed not earlier than the eleventh century B.C. according to the system of chronology suggested in the *Political History of Ancient India* (16th century according to the chronology of the Purāṇas). The references to Śunaḥ-śepa, Parāśara (Śāktya according to the Anukramaṇī) and Śaṁtanu are too clear to be explained away.

The conclusion at which we have arrived is borne out by linguistic and geographical evidence. All scholars of note refer to the striking coincidence in language between the *Avesta* and the cuneiform inscriptions of the Achæmenian kings (6th century B.C.) on the one hand, and the *Ṛig*

[1] Independent proof of the approximate date of Viśvāmitra and his adopted son and pupil Śunaḥ-śepa (Devarāta), and consequently of the hymns composed by them, is furnished by the list of teachers at the end of the *Sāṅkhāyana Āraṇyaka* according to which Viśvāmitra and Devarāta are 15th and 14th respectively in the ascending line from Guṇākhya Śāṅkhāyana, and about six or seven generations removed from Tura Kāvasheya, and Janamejaya Pārikshita. This would place them about two centuries before the age of Parikshit (9th century B. C. according to the system of chronology suggested in the *Political History of Ancient India* and 14th century B.C. according to the Purāṇas).

Veda on the other. Prof. Winternitz admits that the two languages, Old Persian and Old High Indian, are so closely related that it is not difficult to translate the Old Persian inscriptions right into the language of the Veda. In view of this fact we cannot lightly dismiss the testimony of those Vedic texts according to which some of the personages mentioned in the *Ṛig Veda* flourished only about half a dozen generations earlier than Parikshit.

Again, though it may be conceded that the geographical conditions as reflected in the hymns of the *Rig Veda* point to a higher antiquity than those described in the *Brāhmaṇas*, yet there is sufficient evidence to show that the two cannot well be separated by thousands of years. In the time of the *Ṛig Veda* Aryan settlements had spread as far as the country of the Chedis and the river Sarayu the association of which with the Ārya Chitraratha [1] suggests that the river which flows past Ayodhyā is meant. If the story in the *Śatapatha Brāhmaṇa* regarding the spread of Aryan culture to Videha has any value then it cannot be denied that Videha was colonised within a generation after the *Ṛig Vedic* period, for Gotama Rāhūgaṇa,[2] one of the pioneers of Vedic culture in Videha

[1] Ṛig Veda, iv. 30. 18; Rāmāyaṇa, ii. 32. 17.

[2] Ṛig Veda, i. 78.5 ; Sat. Br., i. 4. 1. 10, etc.; xi. 4.3.20.

as well as Namī Sāpya, king of Videha[1] are mentioned in the *Ṛig Veda.* The name of Vidarbhī Kauṇḍinya, fourth in spiritual succession from Ayāsya, presupposes the spread of Aryan civilisation to Vidarbha within four generations from the *Ṛig Vedic* period. The mention of Bhîma Vaidarbha as fourth in spiritual succession from the *Ṛig Vedic* king Somaka, son of Sahadeva,[2] in the *Aitareya Brāhmaṇa* points to the same conclusion.

It may, however, be asked that if the *Ṛig Vedic* Aryans and their proximate successors spread as far as Videha in the east and Vidarbha in the south, how are we to account for the absence of any reference to such well-known *Janapadas* as Kuru, Pañchāla, Śūrasena, Kosala and Magadha in the *Ṛig Veda?*

Now, in the first place it may be pointed out that the *Ṛig Veda* is not a geographical manual, and too much importance should not be attached to the *argumentum ex silentio.* The famous river hymn of the tenth *Maṇḍala* which shows an intimate acquaintance with the whole country from the Gaṅgā to the Kubhā, and mentions even insignificant streams like the Marudvṛidhā, Ārjīkīyā and Sushomā, omits to mention the Dṛishadvatī, Vipāś and Suvāstu. But that these were well-known to the *Ṛig Vedic* poets is clear from other

1 Pañchaviṁśa Brāhmaṇa, xxv. 10.17; Ṛig Veda, vi. 20. 6; x. 48.9.

2 R.V., iv. 15. 7-8.

passages. The *Atharva Veda* certainly knows the Aṅgas and the Magadhas but never refers to the Ganges, the Śoṇa and the Champā. Hiuen Tsang in his account of Mathurā and the surrounding district does not refer to the Jumna. All these show the dangers of the *argumentum ex silentio*. Moreover, it should not be forgotten that all the recensions of the *Rik Saṁhitā*[1] have not come down to us. We have instances in which names omitted in one recension do occur in another recension of the same work (*cf.* the mention of the Kāśis in the *Paippalāda* recension of the *Atharva Veda*). But we need not pursue the matter further because the *Ṛig Veda* actually refers to the peoples called Kurus, Pañchālas, Śūrasenas, Kosalas and Magadhas though under different names, *viz.*, Bharatas, Krivis, Yadus, Āryas on the banks of the Sarayu, and Kîkaṭas respectively. The territorial and racial connexion between the Bharatas and the Kurus is established both by epic and Vedic evidence.[2] Moreover, the name Kuru itself seems to be alluded to in the appellations Kuru-śravaṇa and Kaurayāṇa. As to the Krivis, their identity with the Pañchālas is proved by the testimony of the *Śatapatha Brāhmaṇa* (xiii. 5. 4. 7). The Dālbhyas, a well-known Pañchāla family,[3] are

1 *Cf.* Vishṇu Purāṇa, iii. 4.

2 R.V., iii. 23. 2-4; Śat. Br., xiii. 5. 4. 11. 21; Oldenberg, Buddha, pp. 409-410.

3 Jaiminîya Up. Br., iii. 29. 1.; iv. 7.2.

expressly mentioned in the *Ṛig Veda* in connexion with the river Gomatî (v. 61. 17-19), and it need not be pointed out that a river called Gomatî flows past Rohilkhand, ancient Uttara Pañchāla. That the Yadus were in the *Madhyadeśa* or the "Middle Country" watered by the Upper Ganges and its tributaries, appears probable from their connexion with the Turvaśas and the river Sarayu.[1] The position of the Turvaśas is determined by their connexion with the Yakshus[2] of the Jumna valley[3] with the Pañchālas[4] and the allied tribe of the Sṛiñjayas.[5] A Ṛig Vedic passage (v. 52. 17) seems even to suggest a reference to the famous Gokul on the Jumna so well-known in Purāṇic legends about the Yadus and the Śūrasenas. As to the Āryas on the banks of the Sarayu,[6] one of them, the Ārya Chitraratha is actually mentioned as a *Sachiva* of the Ikshvākus of Ayodhyā in the *Rāmāyaṇa*. The Ikshvākus themselves are referred to in *R. V.*, x. 60. 4. Regarding the Kîkaṭas the only evidence that is available, *viz.*, the evidence of the *Bhāgavata Purāṇa* (i. 3. 24; with Śrīdhara's commentary), the *Bṛihad-dharma Purāṇa* (xxvi 20f), the *Abhidhāna Chintāmaṇi*, etc., identifies them with

1 R.V., iv. 30, 17-18.

2 R.V., vii. 18.6.

3 R.V., vii. 18.19.

4 Sat. Br., xiii. 5. 4. 16.

5 R.V., vi. 27.7.

6 R. V., iv. 30. 18.

the people of Magadha, the scene of Buddha's enlightenment. And it is not unreasonable to prefer the unanimous testimony of mediaeval works to twentieth century guesses.

We have tried to adduce some evidence regarding the approximate date of some of the hymns of the *Ṛig Veda*. Do the Vedic texts furnish any clue as to the date of the foundation of any of the Aryan kingdoms in India? Now, a passage of the *Śatapatha Brāhmaṇa* refers to a Sṛiñjaya king named Dushtarîtu whose realm had existed only for ten generations, and who was a contemporary of the Kuru chief Balhika Prātipīya. It is not unreasonable to infer from this that the foundation of the Sṛiñjaya kingdom took place ten generations earlier than the time of Balhika Prātipīya whom the Great Epic consistently represents as a brother of Śaṁtanu. The Sṛiñjayas are, as is well-known, one of the most famous tribes of the *Ṛig Veda*. Even if we allow the high figure of thirty years for a generation, we cannot place the foundation of the kingdom of this *Ṛig Veda* people before the fourteenth century B. C. according to the system of chronology suggested in the *Political History of Ancient India* and nineteenth century B.C. according to the chronology of the Purāṇas. Thus the date of the rise of one at least of the *Ṛig Vedic* kingdoms cannot possibly be pushed farther back than the second millennium B.C.

CHAPTER II

The Mahābhārata and the Besnagar Inscription of Heliodoros

The Besnagar Inscription records the erection of a *Garuḍa-dhvaja* of Vāsudeva, the god of gods, by the *Bhāgavata* Heliodora (Heliodoros), the son of Diya (Dion), the Takhkhasilāka (native of Taxila), a *Yona* (Greek) ambassador, who came from Mahārāja Aṁtalikita (Antialkidas) to Rājan Kāsiput(r)a Bhāgabhadra the Saviour (*trātāra*), who was prospering in the fourteenth year of his reign.

As this inscription is one of the earliest records of the *Bhāgavatas*, *i.e.*, the followers of Vāsudeva-Kṛishṇa, it is interesting to inquire in what relation it stands to the Great Epic which calls itself the *Kārshṇa Veda*.[1]

At the outset, I beg to draw the attention of scholars to the remarkable passage which forms the second part of the famous epigraph. It runs as follows :—

Trini amuta padāni (su) anuṭhitāni
nayaṁti svaga dama chāga apramāda.

"Three immortal precepts when practised lead to heaven—Restraint, Renunciation and Vigilance."

[1] Mbh., I. 1. 268; xviii., 5.41.

So far as I know no serious attempt has yet been made to find out the source from which these precepts are taken. In my *Early History of the Vaishṇava Sect* I pointed out that *dama, tyāga* and *apaiśunam* are inculcated in the *Gītā*, xvi. 1-2. But *apaiśunam* can hardly be regarded as equivalent to *apramāda*. There are, however, a few verses in the *Strî-parva* (7. 23-25) of the *Mahābhārata* which show a closer resemblance to the passage of the Besnagar inscription. The verses are quoted below :—

Damastyāgo'pramādaścha te trayo Brahma-
ṇo hayāḥ
śīlaraśmi samāyuktaḥ sthito yo mānase rathe
tyaktvā mṛityubhayaṁ rājan Brahmalokaṁ
sa gachchhati

" Restraint, Renunciation and Vigilance—these are the three horses of Brahman. He who rides on the car of his soul, to which are yoked these horses with the help of reins furnished by good conduct, goes, O King, to the regions of Brahma, shaking off all fear of death."

No one can help being struck by the remarkable coincidence between the epic verses and the epigraphic passage mentioned above. *Dama, tyāga* and *apramāda* are mentioned in identical terms in both. "*Amutapadāni*" of the Besnagar Inscription has its parallel in the expression "*tyaktvā mrityubhayaṁ* " of the *Mahābhārata*, while *Svaga* of the epigraph corresponds to Brahmaloka of the epic. It is clear that there was some close connection between the teaching of the *Mahābhārata* and that of the Besnagar Inscription.

There is another important fact which should not be overlooked. Heliodoros, the Greek ambassador to whom we owe the inscription, was a native of Takshaśilā (Taxila) in Gandhāra. The city of Takshaśilā figures prominently in the story of the recitation of the *Mahābhārata*. It was at this city that Janamejaya heard from Vaiśampāyana the famous story of the Kurus and the Pāṇḍus. This is clear from the following verses of the *Svargārohaṇa-parva* :—

Vaiśampāyana uvācha :

Etat te sarvamākhyātaṁ vistareṇa mahādyute
Kurūṇāṁ charitaṁ kritsnaṁ Pāṇḍavānāñcha Bhārata

Sautir uvācha :

etachchhrutvā dvijaśreshṭhāḥ sa rājā Janamejayaḥ
vismito'bhavad atyarthaṁ yajñakarmāntareshvatha
tataḥ samāpayāmāsuḥ karma tat tasya yājakāḥ
Āstīkaśchābhavat prītaḥ parimokshya bhujaṅgamān
tato dvijātīn sarvāṁstān dakshiṇābhir atoshayat

pūjitāśchāpi te rājñā tato jagmuryathāgatam
visarjayitvā viprāṁstān rājāpi Janamejayaḥ
tatas Takshaśilâyâḥ sa punarāyād Gajāhvayam.

(Mbh. xviii. 5. 30-34.)

Vaiśampāyana said:

I have now told you, O you of great splendour, everything about the acts, O Bhārata, of both the Kurus and the Pāṇḍavas.

Sauti said:

Hearing this, O foremost of twice-born ones, at the intervals of sacrificial rites, King Janamejaya became filled with wonder.

The sacrificial priests then finished the rites which remained to go through. Āstîka, having rescued the snakes (from a fiery death) became filled with joy.

King Janamejaya then pleased all the Brāhmaṇas with profuse presents. Thus adored by the king, they returned to their respective abodes.

Having dismissed those learned Brāhmaṇas, king Janamejaya *returned from Takshaśilā to Hāstinapura.*

(M. N. Dutt, Śāstrī's translation.)

The last statement shows that the king was at Takshaśilā (Taxila) when Vaiśampāyana was reciting the story of the Kurus and the Pāṇḍus. It is thus apparent from internal evidence that

Takshaśilā had something to do with the diffusion of the knowledge of Vaiśampāyana's version of the Great Epic. It is significant that one of the earliest references to the *Mahābhārata* is found in the *Ashṭādhyāyī* of Pāṇini, a native of Śālātura which lay not far from Takshaśilā and formed part of the kingdom of Gandhāra.

The testimony of Pāṇini shows that the *Mahābhārata* was well known to the people of Gandhāra from a period long anterior to the time of Heliodoros (second century B.C.), while the evidence of the *Svargārohaṇa-parva* suggests that it used to be recited by Vāchakas or Pāṭhakas in the presence of the great men of Takshaśilā (Taxila). In view of this fact, and of the remarkable coincidence between the verses of the *Strî-parva* of the *Mahābhārata* and the second part of the Besnagar Inscription, it is not unreasonable to think that Heliodoros of Taxila actually heard and utilised the teaching of the Great Epic. Evidently the *Mahābhārata* played an important part in the Hinduisation of the foreign settlers of the Indian borderland.

CHAPTER III

Inter-relation of the Two Epics of Ancient India

There has been considerable misconception regarding the inter-relation of the two famous epics of Ancient India, *viz.*, the *Rāmāyaṇa* and the *Mahābhārata*. Thus Professor Macdonell observes in his *Sanskrit Literature*: "The original part of the *Rāmāyaṇa* appears to have been completed at a time when the epic kernel of the *Mahābhārata* had not as yet assumed definite shape. For while the heroes of the latter are not mentioned in the *Rāmāyaṇa*, the story of Rāma is often referred to in the longer epic. Again, in a passage of Book VII of the *Mahābhārata* which cannot be regarded as a later addition, two lines are quoted as Vālmîki's that occur unaltered in Book VI of the *Rāmāyaṇa*. The poem of Vālmîki must, therefore, have been generally known as an old work before the *Mahābhārata* assumed a coherent form. In Book III (cantos 277-291) of the latter epic, moreover, there is a *Rāmopākhyāna* or 'Episode of Rama,' which seems to be based on the *Rāmāyaṇa*."

In the passage quoted above Professor Macdonell gives three reasons in support of his statement that the poem of Vālmîki was known as an old work before the *Mahābhārata* assumed a coherent form, namely, the absence of any reference to Bhārata heroes in the *Rāmāyaṇa*, the occurrence of a *śloka* of Vālmîki in the Droṇaparva and the inclusion of a *Rāmopākhyāna* within the Great Epic.

Now it is difficult to endorse the view that the heroes of the *Mahābhārata* are not mentioned in the Lesser Epic. The *Uttarākāṇḍa* of the *Rāmāyaṇa* is full of passages which contain undoubted references to characters of the Great Epic. Thus in *Uttara*, lxiii. 20-22, we have a reference to Vāsudeva of the Yadu family, *i.e.*, Kṛishṇa and also to the incarnation of Nara, *i.e.*, Arjuna Pāṇḍava :—

Utpatsyate hi loke'smin Yadūnāṁ kīrtivardhanaḥ
Vāsudeva iti khyāto Vishṇuḥ purusha-vigrahaḥ
sa te mokshayitā śāpād rājaṁstasmād bhavishyasi
kṛitā cha tena kālena nishkṛitiste bhavishyati
bhārāvataraṇārthaṁ hi Nara-Nārāyaṇāvubhau
utpatsyete mahāvīryau Kalau yuge upasthite.

The following verses (*Uttara*, xxiv. 32-42) mention Śyāma (Kṛishṇa) and refer to his victory over Kaṁsa :—

Ya esha purushaḥ śyāmo dvāre tishṭhati nityadā
etena dānavendrāścha tathānye balavattarāḥ
vaśaṁ nītā balavatā pūrve pūrvatarāścha ye
Yamalārjunau cha Kaṁsaścha Kaiṭabho Madhunā saha.

Rādheya and Hārddikya of the following verse probably refer to Karṇa and Kṛitavarman respectively (*Uttara.* vi. 35) :—

Rādheya bahumāyācha lokapālo'tha dhārmikaḥ
Yamalārjunau cha Hārddikyaḥ Śumbhaśchaiva Niśumbhakaḥ.

Dhaumya, the priest of the Pāṇḍavas (Mbh. iii. 3. 1-4) appears to be mentioned in *Uttara*, 1.4 :—

Nṛishaṅguḥ Kavashī Dhaumyaḥ Kauśeyaścha mahān rishih.

The association of Dhaumya with Kavashī is significant. In the *Aitareya Brāhmaṇa* (*Vedic Index*, I, p. 314) and the *Bhāgavata Purāṇa*, Tura Kāvasheya appears as a *Purohita* of Janamejaya, son of Parikshit, whose connection with the Pāṇḍu family is well-known (*cf.* Janamejayah Pāndaveyo, *Mbh.*, I. 38. 2).

It may be argued that the *Uttara-kāṇḍa* is a later addition. But references to *Mahābhārata* characters are not confined to this book. The *Ādi-kāṇḍa* (xl. 2-3) mentions Vāsudeva and his Kāpila-rūpa, *i.e.*, incarnation as Kapila.

Yasyeyaṁ vasudhā kṛitsnā Vāsudevasya dhīmataḥ
mahishī Mādhavasyaishā sa eva bhagavān prabhuḥ
Kāpilaṁ rūpamāsthāya dhārayatyaniśaṁ dharām.

The *Ayodhyā-kāṇḍa* (lxiv. 42) alludes to King Janamejaya along with several famous kings of bygone times such as Sagara, Śaibya, Dilîpa, Nahusha and Dhundhumāra. This Janamejaya must be identified with the famous son of Parikshit and not with any of the shadowy Janamejayas mentioned in some genealogical lists.

The following verse of the same book (xxx. 6) contains a reference to the principal characters of one of the finest episodes of the Great Epic :—

Dyumatsena-sutaṁ vīraṁ Satyavantam anuvratām
Sāvitrîmiva māṁ viddhi tvam ātmavaśavartinîm.

Satyavat and Sāvitrî are again mentioned in the Sundara-kāṇḍa (xxiv. 11-12) which also refers to the principal characters of the Nala episode :—

Sāvitrî Satyavantañcha Kapilaṁ Śrîmatî yathā
Saudāsaṁ Madayantî cha Keśinî Sagaraṁ yathā
Naishadhaṁ Damayantî cha Bhaimî patimanu-vratā
tathāham Ikshvākuvaraṁ Rāmaṁ patimanuvratā.

The *Kishkindhyā-kāṇḍa* (xlii. 28) alludes to the acquisition of the famous śaṅkha of Kṛishṇa called *Pāñchajanya*, while the *Laṅkā-kāṇḍa* (cxix. 15-27) identifies Kṛishṇa with Rāma :—

Tatra Pañchajanaṁ hatvā Hayagrîvañcha dāna-vam
ājahāra tataśchakraṁ śaṅkhañcha Purushottamaḥ
(Kish. xlii. 28.)
Śārṅga-dhanvā Hṛishīkeśaḥ purushaḥ purusho-ttamaḥ.

ajitaḥ khaḍga-dhṛig Vishṇuḥ Kṛishṇaśchaiva Bṛihadbalaḥ.
(Laṅkā, cxix. 15.)
Sītā Lakshmîr bhavān Vishṇur devaḥ Kṛishṇaḥ Prajāpatiḥ.
(*ibid*, cxix. 27.)

The *Laṅkā-kāṇḍa* further seems to refer to the famous episode of the uplifting of Mount Govardhana :—

Parigṛihya giriṁ dorbhyāṁ vapur Vishṇor viḍambayan.
(Laṅkā, lxix. 32 ; *cf*. Mbh. ii. 41.9.)

From the verses quoted above it is clear that the poem of Vālmīki is acquainted not only with some of the principal characters of the Pāṇḍu story, but also with the heroes and heroines of some of the finest *Upākhyānas* of the Great Epic. It may no doubt be argued that the verses in question are late interpolations, but such may also be the case with passages of the Great Epic which contain references to the Rāma story. Professor Macdonell does not assign any reason why the passage of the *Droṇa-parva* which quotes two lines of Vālmîki's poem cannot be regarded as a later addition. As the *Śloka* of Vālmîki occurs in a book which was " much expanded " (Hopkins, *The Great Epic of India*, p. 62), it is not improbable that it is to be included in the " outer layer " of the Great Epic, *i.e.*, the interpolated portions (*ibid*, p. 79).

As regards the *Rāmopākhyāna* we should note that the version of the Rāma story contained in it differs in many respects from that contained in Vālmîki's poem. The *Rāmāyaṇa* (*Uttara*, ix. 33-35) represents Rāvaṇa, Kumbhakarṇa, Śūrpaṇakhā and Vibhîshaṇa, as children of one and the same mother, Kaikasī. The *Rāmopākhyāna* (*Mbh.*, iii. 274. 7-8), on the other hand, makes Rāvaṇa and Kumbhakarṇa sons of Pushpotkaṭā, Vibhîshaṇa, the son of Mālinî, and Khara and Śūrpaṇakhā, the children of Rākā. Again the *Rāmāyaṇa* (vi. 7) represents Rāma as the destroyer of Kumbhakarṇa. On the other hand, the *Rāmopākhyāna* (*Mbh.*, iii. 26) represents Lakshmaṇa as the slayer of Kumbhakarṇa. These facts seem to indicate that the *Rāmopākhyāna* is not based on the *Rāmāyaṇa*. Like the author of the *Dasaratha Jātaka*, the author of the *Rāmopākhyāna* may have followed an independent tradition. In this connection we should remember that Vālmîki was probably not the first to attempt a Rāma Epic. A verse of the *Buddha-charita* of Aśvaghosha possibly records an unsuccessful attempt made by Chyavana, a predecessor of Vālmîki, to write the famous poem which was to make the name of his illustrious descendant immortal.

Vālmîki-nādaścha sasarja padyaṁ
jagraṁthayanna Chyavano Maharshiḥ.

We learn from the *Mahābhārata* (1. 6. 4.) that Chyavana had the patronymic Bhārgava. Curiously enough the *Śānti-parva* of the *Mahābhārata* (lvii. 40) cites a verse from Bhārgava's *Rāma-charita*. No doubt Vālmîki, too, is called Bhārgava-sattamaḥ in the *Matsya Purāṇa* (xii. 51). But the verse cited in the *Śānti-parva* is not found in his poem, though it agrees *in sense* with *Rāmāyaṇa* ii. 67. 11. Some scholars, however, read *Rāja-charita* in the place of *Rāma-charita* and identify its author with Uśanas who was also a Bhārgava. But the fact that Vālmîki had his precursors is proved conclusively by the evidence of the *Ādi-kāṇḍa* which tells us that the *Ākhyāna* called *Rāmāyaṇa* first originated with the Ikshvāku family and that Vālmîki knew Rāma only by hearsay :—

Ikshvākūnām idaṁ teshāṁ rājñāṁ vaṁśe mahātmanām
mahad utpannam ākhyānaṁ Rāmāyaṇam iti śrutam.
(Ādi. V. 3.)

Ikshvāku-vaṁśaprabhavo Rāmo nāma janaiḥ śrutaḥ.
(Ādi. i. 8.)

Hopkins (*The Great Epic of India*, p. 60) draws our attention to the fact that neither of the two epics of Ancient India is recognised before the period of the *Gṛihya-sūtras*, and the first epic recognised here and in other *sūtras* is the *Bhārata*. But he says (p. 385) that the oldest heroes of the *Bhārata* are not of the Pāṇḍu family. He draws a distinction between the original *Bhārati-kathā* and the Pāṇḍu story and says that the *Bhārati-kathā* is older than Vālmīki's poem, but the story of Rāma is older than the story of the Pāṇḍus (*The Great Epic of India*, p. 64). We should, however, remember that Janaka and Aśvapati Kekaya, two important figures in the Rāma story as given by Vālmīki, are represented in several Vedic works as flourishing long after the Pārikshitas, *i.e.*, the great-grandsons of the principal hero of the *Mahābhārata*. In the time of the Vedic Janaka the life and end of the Pārikshitas were, as pointed out by Weber, still fresh in the memory of the people and formed a subject of general curiosity. In the *Bṛihadāraṇyaka Upanishad* (iii. 3.1) we find Bhujyu Lāhyāyani testing Yājñavalkya, the ornament of the court of Janaka, with a question the solution of which the former had previously obtained from Sudhanvā Āṅgirasa, a *Gandharva*, who had in his possession the daughter of Kāpya Patañchala of the Madra territory :—

" *Kva Pārīkshitā'bhavan* ?"

" Whither have the Pārikshitas gone? " The solution of which, therefore, appears to have been looked upon as extremely difficult. Yājñavalkya answers "Thither where all *Aśvamedha* sacrificers go."

The Pārikshitas are Janamejaya and his three brothers, *viz.*, Ugrasena, Bhīmasena and Śrutasena (*Vedic Index*, I, p. 520). They are mentioned in the following passage of the *Mahābhārata* :—

> *Janamejayaḥ Pārīkshitaḥ saha bhrātṛibhiḥ Kurukshetre dīrghasatramupāste tasya bhrātarastrayaḥ Śrutasena-Ugraseno Bhīmasena iti.*
> (Mbh., 1.3.1.)

The Great Epic represents them as grandchildren of Abhimanyu, a prominent figure in the Pāṇḍu story.

It seems probable from what has been stated above that the Rāma story in which Janaka and Aśvapati Kekaya are prominent figures could not have originated before the passing away of the Pārikshitas, *i.e.*, Janamejaya and his brothers. This conclusion is confirmed by the fact that Janamejaya is mentioned as an ancient hero in the Rāmāyaṇa itself (*Ayodhyā-kāṇḍa*. 64.42) :—

> *Yāṁ gatiṁ Sagaraḥ Śaibyo Dilīpo Janamejayaḥ*
> *Nahusho Dhundhumāraścha prāptā-*
> *stāṁ gachchha putraka.*

On the other hand it is distinctly stated in the *Mahābhārata* that the Pāṇḍu story was older than that of Janamejaya, and was in fact recited before Janamejaya by Vaiśampāyana. Indian tradition, both Hindu and Buddhist, is unanimous in representing the Pāṇḍus as an offshoot of the Kuru race.[1] It is, therefore, impossible to justify the distinction drawn by Hopkins between the original Kuru-Bhārata Epic and the so-called "Pāṇḍu story." Hopkins himself admits in the *Cambridge History of India*, Vol. I, p. 253, that "A *Mahābhārata* without Pāṇḍus is like an Iliad without Achilles and Agamemnon; we know of no such poem."

The broad fact remains that while the *Bhārata* is mentioned in the *Gṛihya-sūtras* and the *Ashṭādhyāyī* of Pāṇini, there is no reference to the *Rāmāyaṇa*. Again, while the Pāṇḍu story is said to have been recited before Janamejaya, the Rāma story as given by Vālmîki, containing as it does references to Janaka and Aśvapati Kekaya, could not have originated before the passing away of the Pārikshitas, *i.e.*, Janamejaya and his brothers. There were, of course, many Janakas. But the synchronism of Janaka of the *Rāmāyaṇa* with Aśvapati, or the two Aśvapatis, father and brother of Kaikeyî, probably suggests that Vālmîki had in his mind the famous Janaka of the Upanishads.

PART II

GEOGRAPHY

PART II

Geography

CHAPTER IV

THE STUDY OF ANCIENT INDIAN GEOGRAPHY

For an intelligent study of the history of any country, a thorough knowledge of its geography is indispensable. It is impossible for the student to follow the course of events unless he has accurate information about the precise location of the various places which figure prominently in the narrative. Besides, no scientific historian of a country can overlook the immense influence which its physical features exercise over the character of its people and their political destiny. If the above remarks are applicable to modern history, they apply with still greater force to the ancient history of a country like India with its references to tribes, territories, rivers, mountains and cities whose names have long passed out of current use. Indeed, in the case of India it is not merely the political historian who finds a knowledge of geography to be absolutely essential. The student of social history who reads about the distinctive usages of *Udīchya*, *Śishṭadeśa* and *Dakshiṇāpatha* in the Dharma Sūtras will find it difficult to follow the text unless he knows the exact signification of those terms. The student of literary history must learn to distinguish between *Gauḍa* and *Vidarbha*, *Mahārāshṭra* and *Śūrasena*, to name only a few provinces which gave their names to distinct styles of poetic composition and different kinds of popular speech. More than the political, social and literary historian, the student of religion and mythology will feel at every step the need of a thorough acquaintance with the divine rivers and mountains which receive to this day the homage of the faithful, and those *Dharma-kshetras* and *Puṇya-sthānas* which even now attract pilgrims from the remotest corners of the country. A knowledge of space, no less than that of time, of geography no less than that of chronology, is an indispensable prerequisite of a serious historical study. It is, therefore, needless to emphasise the necessity of the study of the historical geography of Ancient India.

The original materials for the study of Ancient Indian geography are supplied principally from the following sources :—

(1) Indigenous texts on geography.

(2) Incidental references extracted from Indian works of a non-geographical character.

(3) Inscriptions and coins.

(4) Foreign accounts.

(1) Independent Indian treatises dealing with geography are by no means common. A list of such works is given by Mr. S. N. Majumdar Śāstrī in the *Indian Antiquary*, 1921, p. 123. But they have not been sufficiently examined and it is difficult to say how many of them may be accepted as genuine. Compositions of a geographical character are, however, not unoften found embedded in the religious, legendary and astrological literature of Ancient India. One of the earliest and most remarkable compositions of this type is the famous river hymn of the Ṛig Veda (x. 75). No less remarkable are the sections of the Atharvaveda (xix. 17. 1-9) and the Aitareya Brāhmaṇa (viii. 14) referring to the five-fold division of India. Fuller details are given in the two great epics, each of which contains a number of chapters which give a fairly accurate description of India with its territorial divisions. In the Rāmāyaṇic account, for instance, of the search parties of monkeys sent in quest of Sītā, given in four cantos (40-43) of the *Kishkindhyā kāṇḍa*, we have a detailed survey of the tribes, rivers, towns and hermitages of the five great regions of India. In the *Dig-vijaya* and *Tīrtha-yātrā* sections of the sister epic we have details of a similar character. More professedly geographical are the *Jambu-khaṇḍa-vinirmāṇa Parva* (Mbh., vi. 5-9) of the Mahābhārata and the corresponding sections of the Purāṇas and the Kāvya-mīmāṃsā styled

Jambudvīpa-varṇana, *Bhuvana-kośa* or *Bhuvana-vinyāsa* and *Deśa-vibhāga*. Of the same type but of inferior value, is the *Kūrma-vibhāga* or *Kūrma-niveśa* section of Purāṇic and astrological works like the Mārkaṇḍeya Purāṇa (ch. 58), the Bṛihat-saṃhitā and the Parāśara Tantra.[1]

As pointed out by Pargiter [2] "there is plenty of the fabulous in Hindu geography, but it is confined, as a rule, to outside lands and the allusions to purely Indian topography are generally sober." The most serious difficulty in the way of utilising the Epic and Purāṇic accounts is the corruption of the texts. About a thousand years ago Alberuni complained (i. 238) "Such is the custom of the copyists and scribes in every nation. I cannot declare the students of the Purāṇas to be free from it, for they are not men of exact learning." The Bṛihat-saṁhitā is undoubtedly more free from textual corruption. The section called *Kūrma-vibhāga* correctly mentions *Mekalāmbashṭha* and *Puṇḍrotkala* while the corresponding passage of the Mārkaṇḍeya Purāṇa has *Mekhalāmushṭa* and *Purṇotkaṭa*. But, as pointed out by Fleet,[3] the Kurma-vibhāga list "does not furnish materials for preparing an accurate map of Ancient India. Mistakes in details can easily be shown, *e.g.*,

1 *Cf.* also Atharva Pariśishṭa, lvi.
2 J.R.A.S., 1894, p. 231.
3 I.A., 1893, 169f.

though Varāha-mihira places Kachchha and Giri-nagara both in the southern division, he locates Raivataka in the south-west; whereas this mountain is quite close to Giri-nagara (Junāgaḍh) and the Girnār mountain and is considerably to the south of Cutch."

Descriptions of India, and particularly of its central region, are also found in Buddhist literature. Of a slightly different character is the Jaina account of "Milikka" and "Āriya" lands found in the Pannavanā and other Upāṅgas (*cf.* also the Mārkaṇḍeya passage 57, 15. "Tair vimiśrā Janapadā mlechchhāś chāryāś cha bhāgaśaḥ"). The name of the sixth Upāṅga called Jambuddviva-pannatti, however, reminds us of the *Jambudvīpa-varṇana* of the Brāhmaṇical texts.

(2) Besides long texts of a decidedly geographical character, Indian literature, both religious and secular, contains numerous isolated references to countries and cities, rivers and mountains, forests and deserts "which collectively amount to a considerable addition to geographical knowledge." Of special value are the references in the Jātakas, Vinaya texts, the Aṅguttara Nikāya, the Sutta Nipāta, the Mahāgovinda Suttanta, the Dhammapada commentary, the Paramattha-jotikā, the Divyāvadāna, the Mahāvastu, the Jaina Sūtras, the early Tamil poems, the grammatical works of Pāṇini, Patañjali and Krama-dîśvara, the *Kāvyas* of Kālidāsa and Daṇḍin,

the Dharmasūtra of Bodhāyana, the Dharmaśāstra of Manu, the Arthaśāstra of Kauṭilya, the Kāmaśāstra of Vātsyāyana with its commentary, the Nāṭyaśāstra of Bharata, the Siddhānta-śiromaṇi of Bhāskara, Vyāsa's commentary on the *Yoga-sūtras* of Patañjali, and the Rājataraṅgiṇī of Kalhaṇa. Important information is also given in lexicographies like the Amara-kosha, the Abhidhāna-chintāmaṇi and the Abhidhānappadîpikā.

(3) Inscriptions and coins constitute the third class of materials for ancient Indian geography. They are hardly less important to the student of Indian geography than to the student of Indian history. They not only afford us glimpses of the historical map of India in definite epochs, but supplement the information and advance the knowledge derived from literary sources. Who would ever have heard of the kingdoms of Satiyaputra and Ḍavāka, and the province of Vāraka-maṇḍala, but for the inscriptions of Aśoka and Samudra-Gupta and the copper-plate grants of Dharmāditya, Gopachandra and Samāchāradeva? Who would again, have perceived the intimate connection between the city of Madhyamikā and the country of the Sibis but for certain coins discovered near Chitor?

(4) We now turn to the fourth and last class of materials, *viz.*, foreign accounts. Valuable information about India is given by numerous travellers, historians, geographers and even rulers

of foreign nationalities. The name Hindu (Hidu) for instance is first met with in an inscription of a foreign potentate whose dominions extended from the Indus to the Ægean. If we omit the obscure references to Ophir and Sophir (Sovīra or Sauvīra?) in the Bible, the Persians are the earliest foreign people to leave an account of India. Mention is made of this country and some of its rivers and provinces in the Āvestā and the inscriptions of Darius, the potentate to whom we have just referred.

The next foreign people who wrote about India are the Greeks. Writers of this nationality are valuable guides for a period covering about seven centuries from the time of Hekataios to that of Klaudios Ptolemaios. The officers of Alexander and his Seleukidan successors in particular have done much to illumine the darkness enveloping the ancient geography of Northern India, and particularly of the Land of the Five Rivers, the scene of the exploits of 'Philip's warlike son' and his Syrian and Bactrian successors. The Romans and their Greek subjects in Egypt who navigated the Indian ocean and maintained commercial or diplomatic relations with this country in the early centuries of the Christian era, throw much light on the topography of the western seaboard and the land of pepper, pearls and beryls in the Far South. The most valuable additions to our knowledge are made by the author of the Periplus of the Erythræan

Sea and the Christian monk of Alexandria who bore the name of Kosmos Indikopleustes. The store of information gathered by the mariners of the period was evidently utilised by Strabo, Pliny and the compiler of the Peutingerian Tables.

But it is to the Chinese pilgrims, and particularly to Fa-Hien, Song-yun, Yuan Chwang and I-tsing, that we are indebted for the most detailed information about the historic sites of the Indian interior and the countries under its cultural sway. It is a just observation of Cunningham that the pilgrimage of Yuan Chwang "forms an epoch of as much interest and importance for the ancient history and geography of India, as the expedition of Alexander the Great."

The last notable Chinese pilgrim to visit India was U-kong[1] who travelled in the eighth century. It is fortunate that at the time when the light from the Chinese records began to fail, light was vouchsafed from another source, *viz.*, the narratives of Muslim writers. Almost every Muslim observer from Sulaiman to Abul Fazl has something interesting to say about the topography of ancient (and not merely of mediæval) India. The greatest of the Islamic writers is perhaps Al-beruni whose Tahkik-i-Hind was written in 1030 A.D. The account of Al-beruni is valuable not only because it embodies the personal observations of an intelligent foreigner who actually visited this country, but also because it affords us a glimpse into the geographical texts of the Purāṇas available to him, which had already undergone much corruption in his day, *i.e.*, as early as the eleventh century A.D.

The accounts of Muslim writers are supplemented by the records of mediæval European authors like Marco Polo. The Tibetan chroniclers (*cf.* Antiquities of Indian Tibet, p. 64) give little geographical information about the Indian interior that is not available elsewhere.

The known date of most of the foreign writers makes their evidence particularly interesting, and enables the geographer to note the changes in the map of India from age to age. The most serious defect of the non-Indian accounts is the distortion of names due either to the mis-hearing of the Indian sounds or the various transcriptions through which they have come down to us, which makes the work of identification particularly difficult. Another shortcoming which is most noticeable in the work of Klaudious Ptolemaios is the distortion of the shape of India. But this blemish must be shared by those indigenous writers who likened India to a lotus flower or compared its shape to that of a *Kūrma* or tortoise.

A list of pioneers in the field of ancient Indian geographical studies is given by Mr. S. N.

Majumdar Śāstrī in his edition of Cunningham's great work (pp. xvii f.). The following names deserve to be added to the list :—

Edward Thomas, Weber, Bühler, Burgess, Abbott, Holdich, Fleet, Oldham, Rhys Davids, Gerini, Stein, S. Lévi, Foucher, Hultzsch, Kanakasabhai Pillay, Menon, A. Barua, Nobin Chandra Das and Manomohan Chakravarti.

CHAPTER V

Aryan Occupation of India

Indian tradition preserves distinct memories of an earlier home of the Aryans. Thus in the Ṛig Veda, i. 30. 9, a worshipper invokes from his "ancient dwelling place," *Pratnasyaukasaḥ*, the god Indra whom his father formerly invoked. We are also told[1] that *Yadu* and *Turvaśa* were brought by Indra from a distant land, and the former is, in one passage,[2] brought into special relation with *Parśu* (*cf*. Persia). Allusions to tribes and rivers of Irān have been traced in several hymns of the Ṛik Saṁhitā. Hillebrandt, for instance, sees in the Dāsas the Dahæ, and in the Paṇis the Parnians. He finds in the Sarasvatî the Irānian Harahvaitî, identifies the Hariyūpîyā with the river Iryāb or Haliāb and thinks that the Yavyāvatî is the Djob. References to Irān have also been seen in the names Iṣṭāśva[3] (Hystaspes) and Tirindira[4] (*cf*. Tiridates). Post-Vedic tradition indicates that the *Ailas*—a powerful body of Aryans—entered India from the Oxus Valley,

[1] i. 36. 18; vi. 45. 1.

[2] viii. 6. 46.

[3] i. 122. 13.

[4] viii. 6. 46.

from *Bālhi* or *Balhika*, according to the Rāmāyaṇa.[1] This country, it should be noted, finds prominent mention in one of the early Vedic texts, *viz.*, the Atharva Saṁhitā (v. 22, 5. 7, 9). The Papañchasūdanī[2] refers to the establishment of the Kuru Kingdom by a body of colonists from *Uttara-Kuru*, a trans-Himalayan realm known to the Aitareya Brāhmaṇa, the customs of which are quoted for guidance by a Kuru king in the Mahābhārata (Ādi, 122. 7). Whatever we may think of Hillebrandt's suggestions, it is abundantly clear that the horizon of the early Indo-Aryans extended beyond the limits of India and encompassed the plateau of Irān and the tableland of Central Asia. Memories of an ancestral connection with these territories had not faded even in the epic period. But Persia, Bactria and Uttara-Kuru have not yielded the earliest historical traces of Indra-worshipping Aryans. They were probably merely intermediate stages in the Aryan advance towards India. For a still earlier home—for the earliest *historical* notice of Indra-worshipping Aryans—we should perhaps turn to the regions near and beyond the Zagros mountains. An early association of the Indo-Aryans with these regions has been inferred by Tilak and others from words and names like Manā (Ṛig. viii. 78. 2), Taimāta (Atharva V.

[1] Pargiter, *Ancient Indian Historical Tradition*, 254, 299.

[2] Law, *Ancient Mid-Indian Ksatriya Tribes*, p. 16.

18. 4), Urugulā (Atharva v. 13. 8), Yahva (Ṛig. iii. 1. 12; iv. 75. 1; x. 110. 3), as well as from the legend of the flood in the Śatapatha Brāhmaṇa. Recent excavations have disclosed actual traces of a people with Indo-Aryan affinities who lived in Western Asia in the second millennium B.C. The Boghaz-Koi or Boghaz Keui Inscriptions reveal the names of their principal deities, *Mitra*, *Varuṇa*, *Indra* and the heavenly twins, the *Nāsatyas*. The discovery of the name of Indra is of special significance in view of the Ṛig Vedic verses (i. 30. 9; vi. 45. 1) referred to above. Numerals have also been discovered, which are distinctly Indo-Aryan in form. Thus, the form for 1 is *aika-* in a compound, for 3 *teras*, for 5 *panza*, for 7 *satta-*, and for 9 *nāv*.[1] To the same period as the Boghaz-Koi inscriptions belong the famous letters from Tel-el-Amarna. In these occur references to Mesopotamian princes bearing names like *Artatama*, *Tusratta* (*cf.* Daśaratha) and *Suttarna*. In Palestine we come across such names as *Biridashwa* (Sk. *Bṛihadaśva*), *Yashdata* (Yazdāta) and *Shuwardata* (Sk. Sūryadatta). In Babylonia, too, among Kassite princes and deities, we find names like *Maruttash* (Sk. Marut, the wind-god), *Shimalia*, the "lady of the bright mountains" (*cf.* Himālaya), *Dakash*, "star"

[1] *The Cambridge Ancient History*, ii, 13; Childe, *Aryans*, 19.

(*cf. Daksha*, the parent of the Nakshatras of Hindu mythology), and *Shuriyas* "sun" (Sk. *sūrya*).[1]

It is not known for certain when the Aryans first came to North-West India, or rather the Land of the Seven Rivers, *Sapta-Sindhavas* or *Hapta Hindu* as it is called in the Ṛig Veda and the Avestan Vendidad. But their occupation of the country must have taken place at least as early as 1400 B.C.[2]

It seems that the newcomers were at first confined to the Land of the Seven Rivers (including the Sarasvatî, Ṛig. V., vii. 36. 6) and were divided into five tribes.[3] But before the close of the ṚigVedic period they had spread over a vast expanse of territory extending from Eastern Afghanistān to the basin of the Upper Ganges. They had even heard of distant non-Aryan peoples like the *Kîkaṭas* (of Magadha), and of distant non-Aryan strongholds like *Urjayantî* (Ṛig. ii. 13. 8; *cf.* Urjjayanta or the Girnār Hill).

The Aryan occupation of Eastern Kābulistān is proved by the mention of the rivers *Kubhā*

[1] *Cambridge Ancient History*, I, 312, 553. The possible identity of *Dakash* with *Daksha* was suggested by us for the first time in *Cal. Rev.*, 1926, Oct. 124.

[2] See Cal. Rev., 1924, Oct., pp. 67-77.

[3] Pañcha Kshiti, Pañcha Jana, Pañcha Mānusha, Pañcha Krishti. Pañcha Charshani.

(Kābul), *Suvāstu* (Swāt), *Mehatnu*, *Krumu* (Kurram), and *Gomatî* (Gumal), as well as tribes like the *Pakthas* (Pakthūn) and the *Gandhāris* (of the Peshāwar District). Farther east, the Ṛig Vedic people occupied almost the whole of the Pañjāb watered by the *Sindhu* (Indus) and its famous tributaries, the *Sushomā* (Sohān), the *Ārjîkîyā* (probably the Kansi), the *Vitastā* (Jhelum), the *Asiknī* (Chināb), the *Parushṇî* (Rāvi), the *Vipāś* (Bias) and the *Śutudrî* (Sutlaj). Tribes like the Pūrus and the Sivas occupied the country as late as the time of Alexander. In the north the Aryans held a part at least of the secluded vale of Kaśmîra and in the hymns we find mention of the small Kaśmîrian stream, the *Marudvṛidhā* (Maruwardwan), which flows from north to south and joins the Chināb on its northern bank at Kashtwār (Kistawar).

In the east the Ṛig Vedic Aryans had certainly conquered the fertile plains of Sirhind and Thanesar and reached the holy waters of the Jumna and the Ganges,[1] while adventurers appear to have pushed as far as the banks of the *Sarayu*.[2]

[1] See the reference to the Gaṅgā in Ṛig. x. 75. 5, and vi. 45. 31. *Cf.* also Jahnāvî, i. 116.19, iii. 58.6. Scholars who build weighty theories on the paucity of references to the Ganges should remember that in the Yajus and Atharva Saṁhitās it is *not mentioned* at all.

[2] See *Calc. Rev.*, Oct., 1924, pp. 74, 76, for its identification as well as that of the Gomatî in the Madhyadeśa.

The occupation of a part at least of the *Madhya-deśa* appears certain not only from the mention of lakes like Śaryanāvant, and streams like the Sarasvatī,[1] the Āpayā, the Dṛishadvatî, the Yamunā, the Gaṅgā, the Gomatî (which flowed past the dwelling of the Dālbhyas) and the Sarayu, but also from the mention of well-known *Madhya-deśa* tribes and clans like the *Ruśamas*, *Uśînaras*, *Dālbhyas*, *Sṛiñjayas*, *Matsyas*, *Chedis*, and *Ikshvākus*.[2] Some scholars find references even to the *Kurus* and the *Pañchālas* (*Krivis*). It may, of course, be argued that some of these rivers and tribes are to be located in the Western Pañjāb or even in Irān. But such arguments have seldom been supported by cogent proofs. Due weight has rarely been given to the testimony of the Epics and Purāṇas which has been lightly brushed aside even when there is no strong evidence to the contrary in the Vedas themselves.

In the south, Ṛig Vedic poets refer to a region called the Dakshiṇapadā. The exact signification

[1] All the important epithets of the Ṛig Vedic Sarasvatî are found in connection with the epic river of the same name. *Cf.* Mbh. xiii. 146.17f.

एषा सरस्वती पुण्या नदीनामुत्तमा नदी
प्रथमा सर्व्वसरितां नदी सागरगामिनी ॥

[2] See my *Political History of Ancient India*, 1st ed., pp. 27, 28, 32, 49, 65; Oldenberg, *Buddha*, pp. 401, 403.

of this term is not known. But the absence of any reference to the mountains, rivers and tribes of Central and Southern India makes it unlikely that we have here the earliest historical notice of the Deccan. An acquaintance with the desert of Rājputāna[1] is probably, however, suggested by the constant mention of *Dhanvan*.

With the exception of the territory defined above, the whole of India was occupied by non-Aryan

[1] As to the theory of a "Rājputāna sea" into which the Vedic Sarasvatī is said to have emptied itself, which has been propounded in recent times, we should note that the epithet *Sāgara-gāminī* is applied to the Sarasvatī even in the Epic period when, surely, there was no "Rājputāna sea." As to references to the four Samudras it should be remembered that "*Chatuḥ-Samudra*," "*Chatvāraścha mahārṇavāḥ*" (Mbh. xiii. 150.27), "*Chaturdadhi*" are stock phrases of Sanskrit literature like the 'seven oceans' of Purāṇic mythology (*cf.*, Saptabudhnam arṇavam, Ṛig Veda, viii. 40.5; also IA., 5, 17) and occur even in inscriptions of the Gupta and even post-Gupta (IA., 3, 305) periods. The idea was originally derived from the four quarters of the sky. In the Ṛig Veda (vi. 58. 3: X. 98. 12; 123. 2) we have clear references to the use of the term *Samudra* in the sense of *antariksha* and *dyau*. *Cf.* Yāska's *Nirukta*. ii, 10: "*Ambaram Viyat Vyoma......Samudraḥ* ...." The term *Samudra* was also applied to big rivers like the Ganges as late as the period of the Jātaka commentary (*cf.* Jātaka No. 342). The "sweet water swelling up from the Samudra" (Ṛig. iv, 58.1) cannot refer to the saline water of the sea. Minhāj calls the Begmatī *Sumund* *i.e.*, ocean (Raverty, 561).

tribes. These *Anāryas* are referred to under the general designation of Dāsas or Dasyus. We have also notices of specific tribes like the Śimyus and the Kîkaṭas and probably also the Ajas, Yakshus, and Śigrus.

In the next **period,** *viz.*, that **of the Yajus and Atharva** Saṁhitās, and the earlier Brāhmaṇas, the Aryan occupation of the Gangetic Doāb is completed, and we hear for the first time of flourishing settlements in Central India, on the banks of the Varaṇāvatî, and even farther to the east. Central India was explored by tribes like the Kuntis and the Vîtahavyas who figure prominently in the later Saṁhitās and are associated with the Malwan region in the period of the Great Epic. In the eastward expansion the lead was taken by two tribes, *viz.*, the Bharatas and the Videghas (Videhas). The former advanced along the Yamunā, and the latter across the Sarasvatî and the Sadānîrā (Rāpti or Gaṇḍak). The widening of the eastern horizon is synchronous with an intimate knowledge of the north, and the Bahlikas, Mahāvṛishas, Gandhāris and Mūjavats appear in the Atharva Saṁhitās side by side with the Kāśis, Magadhas and Aṅgas.

The later **Brāhmaṇas, Āraṇyakas and Upanishads** introduce us to a geographical area not much different from that of the later Saṁhitās except in regard to a few particulars. The centre of Aryan civilisation now, as in the earlier epochs of the

Yajus and the Atharva, is found to lie in the Ganges-Jumna region. But we now hear for the first time of the great Dakshiṇa-parvata, *i.e.*, the Vindhya (Kaushîtaki, ii. 8), and the vast territory beyond it, as well as the eastern region beyond the Sadānîrā, peopled by Dasyu tribes, but already partially occupied by the vanguards of Vedic civilisation. We have, moreover, a glimpse of India with its five-fold division :—the Dhruvā-Madhyamā Pratishṭhā diś (the Middle Quarter), the Prāchî diś (Eastern Quarter), the Dakshiṇā diś (Southern Quarter), the Pratîchî diś (Western Quarter), and the Udîchî diś (Northern Quarter). The division is already anticipated by the Atharva Saṁhitā (xix. 17. 1-9), but for detailed information we must turn to the Aitareya Brāhmaṇa. In the Dhruvā Madhyamā diś lay the realms of the Kurus, the Pañchālas, the Vaśas and the Uśînaras. The realms of Prāchî are not specifically named, but we learn from other sources that the following peoples existing in the Brāhmaṇa period belonged to that region, *viz.*, the Kosalas,[1] Kāśis,[2] Videhas, Magadhas and

[1] The Kosalan capital (Sāvatthi) was included in the eastern region (Puratthima Janapada) as late as the time of the Aṅguttara Nikāya (Part I, p. 66). In the *Pratijñā-Pariśishṭa*, Kāmpilya is given as the eastern limit of the *Madhyadeśa* (Weber, *Ind. Lit.*, 115n).

[2] Kāśi is excluded from the Madhyadeśa even by Manu who makes Prayāga the eastern boundary of that region.

Aṅgas. Some scholars find a reference to the Vaṅgas in the Aitareya Āraṇyaka, but the only people of the Far East of India mentioned distinctly in the later Vedic texts are the Puṇḍras. The most important peoples of the Dakshiṇā diś were the Nishadhas, the Satvats, governed by Bhoja kings, and their kinsmen, the Vaidarbhas of Berar.

The Aryan settlements in the South were surrounded by Dasyu tribes like the Andhras, Śavaras, Pulindas and Mūtibas.[1] About the peoples of Pratîchî, namely, the Nîchyas and the Apāchyas, we do not know much. The peoples of Udîchî mentioned specifically by the Aitareya Brāhmaṇa are the Uttara-Kurus and the Uttara-Madras, who dwelt beyond the Himavat ; but the Brāhmaṇa texts give us also names of many other tribes living to the north-west of the Dhruvā Madhyamā diś such as the Gandhāris, or Gandhāras, Kekayas, Madras and Ambashṭhas [2]

The next **period**—that **of the Brāhmaṇical and Buddhist Sūtras**—was marked by a simultaneous advance in two directions, *viz.*, the west and the south. The boundaries of the Madhya-deśa

It is in comparatively recent times that this famous place came to be included within the Madhyadeśa as we learn from the Kāvya-mīmāṁsā.

[1] See my *Political History of Ancient India*, 1st ed , pp. 44-45.

[2] *Ibid*, pp. 23-27, 131.

were enlarged and mention is made of a number of new kingdoms in the west and the south. Moreover, it was in this epoch that the Hindus for the first time referred to a very famous people of antiquity, *viz.*, the Yavanas or the Greeks.[1]

The Dhruvā Madhyamā diś, then called Āryāvarta, the Sishtadeśa, or Majjhima deśa, though still confined by some to the Gangetic Doāb, really embraced a wider area. The Himavat range and particularly the Uśînara Peak were still mentioned as the northern boundary, but the eastern frontier now reached the Kālakavana, probably near Allahabad. The southern boundary was formed by the Pāriyātra, *i.e.*, the Western Vindhyas, and the western boundary by Adarśana and Thuna, both situated on the Sarasvatî. Beyond the western boundary of the Madhya-deśa, Aryan civilisation had spread as far as the Arabian Sea and we hear for the first time of western realms of mixed origin (*Saṅkîrṇa-yonayaḥ*) like Avanti, Surāshṭra, Sindhu and Sauvîra.

In the south the Aryans had overstepped the limits of Vidarbha and spread as far as the Godāvarî. The terms Dakshiṇāpatha and Dākshiṇātya came into prominence and the Godāvarî valley was dotted over with Aryan settlements

[1] The Romans (Romakas) and the Chinese (Chînas) do not appear till the period of the epics, the Kauṭilîya Arthaśāstra, and the Milinda-pañho.

like Pañchavaṭī, Janasthāna, Aśmaka and Mūlaka. The western and eastern sea-boards of the Deccan were also thoroughly explored. On the west coast rose the great ports of Bharukachchha and Śūrppāraka, while the vast region between the Amarkaṇṭaka range and the Bay of Bengal rapidly developed into the populous and powerful kingdom of Kaliṅga. Kaliṅga, however, does not seem to have been an Aryan Kingdom as it is branded as an impure country by Bodhāyana. The southerners observed several customs not approved by the people of the Madhya-deśa, *e.g.*, eating with the uninitiated and with one's own wife, taking stale food, and marrying the daughter of a *mātula* and *pitṛisvashā*.

The whole of the vast territory to the east of Aṅga was still regarded as an impure country, but there was some difference of opinion between the the Brāhmaṇists and Buddhists regarding the Aṅgas and the Magadhas. The Brāhmaṇical sūtras of Bodhāyana regarded them as outside the Madhya-deśa and called them "Saṅkīrṇa-yonayaḥ," the Buddhist Vinaya texts, on the other hand, included these peoples within the Madhyadeśa, which, according to them, extended as far as Kajaṅgala (the Rājamahal Hills). Regarding the regions which lay farther to the east, *viz.*, Puṇḍra, Suhma and Vaṅga, there is no such difference of opinion. The early Pāli canon rarely does the honour of mentioning them. The Jaina Kalpa

Sūtra regards Rāḍha-Suhma as a savage tract. Bodhāyana recommends an expiatory sacrifice after a journey to the Puṇḍras and the Vaṅgas. Even Patañjali, who flourished in the second century B. C., excludes the lower Ganges Valley from Āryāvarta which, according to him, lay to the west of Kālaka-vana.[1] It is not till we come to the Manu-saṁhitā that we find the eastern boundaries of Āryāvarta extended to the sea, *i.e.*, the Bay of Bengal. The first indubitable reference to Vaṅga (including Tāmralipti) as an 'Āriya' land occurs in a Jaina Upāṅga.[2] Prāgjyotisha (Kāmarūpa or Assam) is entirely ignored in the Vedic texts and the early canon of the Jainas and the Buddhists. It first appears in the Epics, but even in the extant Mahābhārata its king Bhagadatta is represented as a leader of barbarian hordes (Mbh., v. 19.15).

The northern region, hallowed by the songs of the Ṛig Veda, was no longer looked upon as a sacred clime and some of its peoples, *e.g.*, the Āraṭṭas, are placed on a level with the impure tribes of the east, *viz.*, the Puṇḍras and the Vaṅgas. The reason is perhaps to be found partly in the observance by the people of these tracts of practices abhorrent to Mid-Indian sentiment, such as dealing in wool, rum-drinking, selling animals that had teeth in the upper and in the lower jaws,

1 Kielhorn's ed., i. 475.
2 *Ind. Ant.*, 1891, p. 375.

following the trade of arms and going to sea, and partly in the influx of foreign intruders like the Persians and the Yavanas.

In the Araṇya and Kishkindhyā Kāṇḍas of the **Ramayana** we see the first beginnings of the Aryan infiltration into the country south of the Godāvari. Though vast tracts of the Deccan were still covered with forests and the main body of Aryan settlers was still confined to the territory lying to the north of the Godāvari, Aryan sages had already opened up the country as far south as the Pampā (possibly the Tuṅgabhadrā), and Aryan princes had pushed as far as Ceylon. The Aryans had not, however, yet come to the far south in large numbers, and, it is not till the days of Kātyāyana and Megasthenes (fourth century B.C.), that we have the first chronologically valuable references to flourishing *Janapadas* in the fertile valleys of the Kāverî and the Tāmraparṇî.

CHAPTER VI

INDIA IN PURĀṆIC COSMOGRAPHY

(The nomenclature of India and the place of the country in the cosmic system of the Hindus)

Early nomenclature of India.

India surrounded on three sides by the great ocean and bounded on the fourth side by the most stupendous mountain system of the world which 'stretches along on its north like the string of a bow' (kārmukasya yathā guṇaḥ)[1] is undoubtedly a geographical unit. But we have no comprehensive designation for the country in the earliest literature, whether Indian or foreign. Neither *Sapta Sindhavaḥ*, the name applied to their home-land by the Vedic Aryans, nor Āryāvarta, the designation of Aryandom in the days of Bodhāyana and Manu, meant the whole of the Indian sub-continent; and even the terms 'Hidus'[2] and 'India'[3] when used by Darius and Herodotus did not probably denote at first any territory beyond the Indus valley. The reason is not far

[1] Mārkaṇḍeya Purāṇa, 57, 59. Pargiter's translation, p. 347.

[2] *Ancient Persian Lexicon and the texts of the Achæmenidan Inscriptions by H. C. Tolman.*

[3] Herodotus, Book III, Chs. 97-98.

to seek. The Indian and foreign peoples to whom we are indebted for the earliest notices of Hindusthān, were acquainted only with one corner of this vast sub-continent, *viz.*, the north-west region watered by the Indus and the upper Ganges. It is only in or about the fourth century B. C. that we have the first indubitable proof—in the pages of Kātyāyana[1] and Megasthenes[2]—of the exploration of the whole country down to the Pāṇḍyan realm in the extreme south.[3] And it is precisely about this period that we have the first clear indication of the use of a comprehensive term for the great territory stretching from the Himavat to the sea. That term is Jambudvîpa.

Jambudvpia—its denotation.

As is well-known, Jambudvîpa is mentioned in one of the minor Rock Edicts of Aśoka[4] as the designation of the extensive region throughout which the *Pakama* (Parākrama) of the Maurya Emperor made itself felt. The term is used to denote the dominions of Aśoka in the seventh century A. D.,

1 Vārttika to Pāṇini, iv. 1, 168 (Pāṇḍor ḍyaṇ).

2 Fragments LI, LVI B, LVIII.

3 There are no doubt references to the Pāṇḍya country in the epics. But these cannot be dated even approximately.

4 Y(i)-imāya kālāya Jambudipasi amisā devā husu te dāni m(i)s kaṭā. Pakamasi hi esa phale.

by I-tsing[1] who clearly distinguishes it from China[2] and mentions Fu-nan or Poh-nan (Kuo) as lying on its south corner.[3] But already in the period of the Epics and the Purāṇas Jambudvîpa has acquired a wider denotation. Though still distinguished from Śākadvîpa—the land of the *Maga dvijas* who worship the sun-god[4]—it is

[1] I-tsing's *Record of the Buddhist Religion*, trans. by Takakusu, p. 14.

[2] *Ibid*, p. 136.

[3] *Ibid*, pp. 12-13. Fu-nan corresponds to Siam and part of Cambodia (Takakusu).

[4] Magā Magadhamānasyā Mandagāścha dvijātayaḥ
yajanti Sūryarūpantu Śākaḥ kshírābdhinā vṛitaḥ
(Agni P., 119. 21).

Magā Brāhmaṇa-bhūyishṭhā Magadhāḥ Kshatriyāstu te
Vaiśyāstu Mānasāsteshāṁ Śūdrā jñeyāstu Mandagāḥ
Śākadvîpe sthitair Vishṇuḥ Sūryarūpa-dharo Hariḥ
yathoktairijyate samyak karmabhir niyatātmabhiḥ
(Brahma P., xx. 71f.).

Cf. Also Kūrma Purāṇa, i, 48. 36-37; Mbh., vi. 11, 8-38. In the epic, however, Śākadvîpa seems to be regarded as a centre of Saivism (pūjyate tatra Śaṅkaraḥ, vi. 11, 28).

The Sun-worshipping Maga Brāhmaṇas are doubtless the Magi of Irāṇ (Bhandarkar, *Vaishṇavism, Saivism and Minor Religious Systems*, p. 153). In the Śaṅkara-worshipping inhabitants of Śākadvîpa we may perhaps find a reference to Scythic Kings like Kadphises II and Vāsudeva I. Note also the presence of the Pāśupatas in "Lang-ka-lo" which was subject to Persia (Watters, ii. 257). Vidyābhūshaṇa identifies Śākadvîpa with Sogdiana (JASB, 1902, Part I, p. 154).

regarded as practically identical with *Kshiti* (the earth), and is described as being "low on the south and north, and highly elevated in the middle" (dakshiṇottarato nimnā madhye tuṅgāyatā Kshitiḥ).[1] Among its divisions we find mention of Ketumāla, the valley of the Vaṅkshu[2] (Oxus), Ilāvṛita, the district round Meru[3] which the Mahābhārata places near the sandy desert beyond the Himālayas,[4] and Uttara-Kuru, another trans-Himālayan tract[5] which has become quite mythical in the Purāṇic period. The Island of Java (Yava) is also included within its limits.[6]

The system of Dvîpas and Varshas.

As the denotation of Jambudvīpa becomes wider need is felt for a new term to mean the country south of the Himavat. Such a term is Bhārata-varsha which,

[1] Mārkaṇḍeya P., Ch. 54. 12 f.

[2] *Ibid*, Ch. 54. 8-14; 56. 13f.; 59. 12-17, Vaṅkshu is often corrupted into Chakshu, Raṅkshu. Sva-rakshu, etc. See Ind. Ant., 1912, p. 265 f.

[3] Madhye tv-Ilavṛito yastu, Mahāmeroḥ samantataḥ (Brahmāṇḍa Purāṇa, Ch. 35. 22).

[4] Mbh., xvii. 2. 1-2,

tataste niyatātmāna Udīchīṁ diśamāsthitāḥ
dadṛiśur yogayuktāścha Himavantam mahāgirim
taṁ chāpyatikramantaste dadṛiśur bālukārṇavam,
avaikshanta mahāśailaṁ Meruṁ śikhariṇāṁ varam.

[5] Pareṇa Himavantam (Aitareya Brāhmaṇa, viii. 14. Vedic Index).

[6] Brahmāṇḍa (52.14-19).

in the opinion of Lüders, is mentioned as early as the Hāthigumphā Inscription of Khāravela, king of Kalinga.[1] Jambudvîpa, however, still continues to be used in its narrower sense as a synonym of Bhārata-varsha.[2] The world is now conceived of as comprising seven concentric island continents (Saptadvîpā Vasumatî[3]) separated by encircling seas[4] which 'increased double and double compared with each preceding one' (dviguṇair dviguṇair vṛiddhyā sarvataḥ pariveshṭitāḥ).[5]

[1] Lüders, List of Brāhmî Inscriptions, No. 1345.

[2] *Cf.* Mbh., vi. 6. 13:

> tasya pārśveshvamî dvîpā
> śchatvāraḥ saṁsthitā vibho
> Bhadrāśvaḥ Ketumālaścha
> Jambudvîpaścha Bhārata.

Cf. also Brahmāṇḍa Purāṇa, 37. 27-46; 43. 32.

[3] Patañjali's Mahābhāshya, Kielhorn's ed., Vol. I, p.9. *Cf.* Sapta-dvîpavatî Mahî (Brahmāṇḍa 37. 13). The number is sometimes raised to nine (sasāgarā navadvîpā dattā bhavati Medinî, Padma, Svarga, vii. 26) or thirteen (trayodaśa samudrasya dvîpānaśnan Purūravāḥ, Mbh., i, 74, 19, with Nīlakaṇṭha's com.) or reduced to four (Mbh., vi. 6. 13).

[4] And apparently floating on them—Jalopari mahî yātā naurivāste sarijjale (Garuḍa, 54. 4).

[5] Mārk. P., Ch. 54.7; Alberuni, 1. 233; *cf.* the Buddhist teaching about the world and the system of which it forms a constituent as summarised by Hiuen Tsang (Watters, Yuan Chwang, I, pp. 31-36): "In the ocean, resting on a gold disk is the mount Sumeru. Around the Sumeru are seven mountains and *seven seas*,

These insular continents ("dry collars" of Alberuni) are further divided into smaller areas (Khaṇḍakān)[1] called *Varshas*,[2] Bhārata being the name of the southernmost *Varsha*[3] of the innermost continent, Jambudvīpa.

As pointed out by Alberuni[4] and Abul Fazl[5] there is considerable diversity in the order of the *Dvîpas* and *Varshas* and their extent and other particulars. There is, however, agreement in regard to the first and seventh Dvîpas which are invariably named Jambu and Pushkara[6] respectively. The names of the *Dvîpas* and seas as given in the Agni and most of the other

Outside the seven gold mountains is the salt sea. In the sea there are four islands, *viz.*, Kuru, Godāna, Videha and Jambu." For Jaina Cosmography, see Barnett, *Antiquities of India*, p. 198 f.

1 For Khaṇḍakān see Garuḍa Purāṇa, Ch. 54. 12-

2 Varsha is thus defined in the Brahmāṇḍa (53, 133-134):—

ṛishayo nivasantyasmin prajā yasmāchchaturvidhāḥ,
tasmād Varshamiti proktam prajānāṁ sukhadantu tat
ṛisha ityeva ṛishayo vṛishaḥ śakti prabandhane.
iti prabandhanāt siddhiṁ varshatvaṁ tena teshu tat.

3 dakshiṇam varsham Himāhvam (Brahmāṇḍa, Ch. 33. 44).

4 Vol. 1, p. 236.

5 *Ain-i-Akbari*, iii. 32 (trans. by Jarrett).

6 dvîpā mayā proktā Jambu-dvîpādayo..Pushkarāntāḥ (Mārk. P., 54-6).

Purāṇas are mentioned below :—

Jambu-Plakshāhvayau dvîpau
Śālmaliśchāparo mahān
Kuśaḥ Krauñchastathā Śākaḥ
Pushkaraścheti saptamaḥ
ete dvîpāḥ samudraistu
sapta saptabhirāvṛitāḥ
lavaṇekshu-surā-sarpir-
dadhi-dugdha-jalaiḥ samam.[1]

Alberuni[2] seems to prefer the evidence of the *Matsya Purāṇa* which, along with the *Padma*, mentions the names in the following order:— Jambu, Śāka, Kuśa, Krauñcha, Śālmali, Gomeda (in the place of Plaksha), and Pushkara.[3] Abul Fazl[4] regards the legends about the six outer continents as being beyond the limits of credibility. So he puts them aside and confines himself to a few particulars regarding Jambudvîpa. It may at once be conceded that the description of most of the seven *dvîpas* in the extant Purāṇas marks them out as things of fairyland,[5] comparable

1 Agni, 108. 1-3.

2 Vol. 1, p. 236.

3 For the enumeration of the dvîpas see Matsya, Chs. 122-123 ; Padma, Svarga-khaṇḍa, Ch. IV.

4 *Ain-i-Akbari*, iii. 29.

5 *Cf*. Vishṇu Purāṇa, II. iv. 9-15, etc.

"nādhayo vyādhayo vāpi sarva-kāla-sukhaṁ hi tat."

"Plaksha-dvîpādishu Brahman Śākadvîpāntikeshu vai pañchavarsha-sahasrāṇi janā jîvantyanāmayāḥ." etc.

to the Isles of the Blessed or the Spanish El Dorado. The very conception of the earth as an aggregate of seven concentric islands surrounded by seas is pure mythology. It is, however, well to remember that the word *dvîpa* originally meant nothing more than a land between two sheets of water [1] (usually rivers), and that some of the Purāṇic dvîpas are obviously named after tribes, or connected with localities, which can be identified with more or less certainty. Śākadvîpa, for example, is obviously named after the Śakas and the description of its inhabitants as 'Maga-dvijas' who worship "*Sūrya-rūpa-dharo Hari*" clearly points to its identification with Śakasthāna or Seistan in Irān, the land of the Magi and of the Mihira cult.[2] Votaries of this cult migrated to India in large numbers probably in the Scythian period and constitute the Śākadvîpî community of the present day.[3] The name of the next dvîpa mentioned in the Matsya Purāṇa, *viz.*, Kuśa, reminds us of the famous race which, according to Kumāralāta and

1 Dvirāpatvāt smṛito dvîpaḥ (Brahmāṇḍa, 53. 140), *Cf.* Mahābhāshya, Kielhorn's ed. Vol. I, p. 131. *Cf.* also Śākaladvîpa mentioned in the Mahābhārata (ii. 26. 5-6) which was clearly a tract between two rivers (the Rāvi and the Chināb).

2 *Cf.* Bhandarkar, *Vaishṇavism, Śaivism and Minor Religious Systems*, p. 153.

3 *Cf.* Bhandarkar (Prof. D. R.), Foreign Elements in the Hindu Population (Ind. Ant.), p. 11. Vidyābhūshaṇa, JASB, 1902, Part I, pp. 152-155.

Baron A. von Staël Holstein,[1] gave India the powerful emperors of Kanishka's line. Plaksha which is placed next to Jambudvîpa by many Purāṇas [2] as well as the commentator of Patañjali,[3] has, as one of its streams, the river Kramu or Krumu [4] mentioned as early as the Ṛig Veda,[5] and identified by scholars with the modern Kurram, a western tributary of the Indus. In one Purāṇic list we find Kubhā (the Kābul river) in place of Krumu.[6] These facts may point to some region immediately to the west of the Indus as the probable site of the 'Plaksha dvîpa' of the Purāṇas.[7] A Purāṇic

[1] JRAS, Jan., 1914, pp. 79-88; Smith, *Early History of India*, 4th ed., p. 266 n. For Kumāralāta, see my *Political History of Ancient India*, 3rd ed., p. 322. Vidyābhūshaṇa (JASB, 1902, Part I, p. 151) compares the *Damin* Brāhmaṇas of Kuśadvîpa (Vishṇu Purāṇa, II, iv. 39) with the Damnai and other tribes inhabiting Serike (Ancient India as described by Ptolemy, ed. S. N. Majumdār, pp. 299, 305).

[2] *Cf.* Plaksha-dvîpa-parikrāntaṁ Jambudvîpaṁ nibodhata (Brahmāṇḍa, 34-40. *Cf.* also 50-4).

[3] Alberuni. Vol. I, p. 235. The Bhāshya on Patañjali's Yoga-sūtras is meant here. It is attributed to Vyāsa.

[4] Brahmāṇḍa, 53.19; Garuḍa, 56.4. 'Anutaptā Śikhî chaiva Vipāśā Tridivā Kramuḥ.'

[5] See *Vedic Index*.

[6] Kūrma Purāṇa, i., Ch. 48.7. 'Anutaptā Śik ā chaiva Vipāpā Tridivā Kubhā.'

[7] Vidyābhūshaṇa is inclined to identify Plaksha-dvîpa with Ariana (JASB, 1902, Part I, p. 151).

passage quoted by Alberuṇi[1] places Pushkara between Chîna and Maṅgala (Mongolia?). Thus the account of the 'seven dvîpas' may have had originally a substratum of reality. But the extant texts bearing on the subject are so hopelessly corrupt that the kernel of truth is in most cases buried beyond reach underneath a vast mass of Utopian myths.[2] It is only in the account of Jambudvîpa that the poet has not altogether thrust out the geographer.[3]

The Varshas of Jambudvîpa.

Jambudvîpa—also called Sudarśanadvîpa—is said to derive its name "from a tree growing in it, the branches

1 Ch. XXV, p. 261.

2 Vishṇu, II, iv. 9-15 quoted above. Compare also the textual corruptions in the account of Śākadvîpa in Brahmāṇḍa, 53.76 f., and Garuḍa, 56, 14-15 ; in Vishṇu, II, iv. 69 f., Maga (=Magi) becomes Mṛiga! *Cf.* also the account of Pushkaradvîpa in Vishṇu, Book II, Ch. IV, 73-93, esp.

"Bhojanam Pushkara-dvîpe tatra svayam upasthitam,
Shaḍrasaṁ bhuñjate vipra prajāḥ sarvāḥ sadaiva hi."

This dvîpa is surrounded by the sea of स्वादूदक (sweet water), beyond which lies the golden earth (Kañchanî bhūmi) which is sarva-jantu-vivarjitā. Behind it lies Lokāloka śaila, a mountain of the height of ten yojanas!!! Bhāskara in the Siddhānta Śiromaṇi "dismisses the system of dvîpas as Paurāṇikî kathā" (Seal, *Vaishṇavism and Christianity*, p. 48).

3 Jambudvîpa is the continent inhabited by human beings, *Jambudvîpo narāśrayaḥ* (Brahmāṇḍa, 37.34).

of which extend over a space of 100 Yojanas."[1] It is said to be shaped like a lotus with Meru as its karṇikā (pericarp) and the *Varshas* or *Mahādvîpas*, Bhadrāśva, Bhārata, Ketumāla and Uttara-kuru, as its four petals.[2] Less poetical, but

[1] For the derivation of the name, see Alberuni, i. 251; Brahmāṇḍa, 37.28-34 ; 50.25-26; Matsya, 114.74-75.

Sudarśano nāma mahān Jambu-vṛikshaḥ sanātanaḥ
tasya nāmnā samākhyāto Jambudvîpo vanaspateḥ
(Matsya), *cf.* Mbh., vi. 5.13-16; vi. 7.19-20.

There was also a river called Jambū nadī which takes the place of Suchakshu (Oxus) in a passage of the Mahābhārata (Hopkins, *Epic Mythology*, p. 5). Is Amu a corruption of Jambū ?

[2] Jambudvîpaśchaturdala-kamalākāraḥ—(Nīlakaṇṭha's Commentary on Mbh., vi. 6.3-5).

tadevam pārthivam padmaṁ chatushpatram mayoditam
Bhadrāśva-Bhāratādyāni patrāṇyasya chaturdiśam
(Mārk., 55, 20f).

Pṛithivîpadmaṁ Maru-parvata-karṇikam
(Brahmāṇḍa, 35.41).

Mahādvīpāstu vikhyātāśchatvāraḥ patrasaṁsthitāḥ
Padma-karṇika-saṁsthāno Merurnāma mahābalaḥ
(*ibid*, 50).

Chaturmahādvîpavatī seyamūrvī prakīrtitā
(Brahmāṇḍa, 44.35).

The names of the "four mahādvîpas" are given in Ch. 35, verses 50-61, and Ch. 44, verses 35-38, as Bhadrāśva, Bhārata, Ketumāla and Uttara-kuru. In Ch. 37, verses 27-46 ; Ch. 43.32 and Mbh., vi. 6.13, Jambudvîpa takes the place of Bhārata, while Buddhist authors replace Bhadrāśva and Ketumāla by Pūrva-videha and

more important from the point of view of sober geography, is the description of Jambudvîpa as being 'low on the south and north, and highly elevated in the middle.'[1] The elevated region in the centre is styled Ilâvṛita or Meru Varsha, *i.e.*, the district round Meru.[2] To the north of this tract lie Ramyaka,[3] Hiraṇmaya[4] and Uttara-kuru[5] and on the south are Bhārata,[6] Kimpurusha[7] and

Apara-godāna respectively (Kern, *Manual of Indian Buddhism*, p. 57; Watters, Yuan Chwang, Vol. I, pp. 31-36). Jambudvîpa according to Buddhist writers is divided by four lords—the elephant-lord who rules the South (India), the lord of precious substances who rules the West (Rome?), the horse-lord who rules the North (Scythia?) and the man-lord who rules the East (China).

1 Mārk., 54.12 f.

2 Meruvarshaṁ mayā proktaṁ madhyamaṁ yad-Ilâvṛitam (Mārk., 60.7). Madhye tv-Ilâvṛito yastu Mahā-meroḥ samantataḥ (Brahmāṇḍa, 35.22).

3 Also called Ramaṇaka (Matsya, 113.61 ; Mbh., vi. 8.2) and Nîlavarsha (Brahmāṇḍa, 34.46). The Garuḍa Purāṇa places it on the north-west of Meru (Ch. 55.3).

4 Hiraṇmayaṁ nāmā yatra Hairaṇvatî nadî (Mbh., vi. 8.5), also called Śvetavarsha (Brahmāṇḍa, 34.46 ; Agni, Ch. 107.7). *Cf.* Śvetadvîpa of the *Nārāyaṇîya*. The Garuḍa Purāṇa places Hiraṇvat in *Pūrva-dakshiṇa* (Ch. 55.1). For the name Hiraṇvat see also Matsya, 113.64.

5 Also called Śṛiṅgavad-varsha (Brahmāṇḍa, 34.47) and Airāvata-varsha (Mbh., vi. 6.37).

6 Also called Himāhva (Brahmāṇḍa, 34.44, 53), Haimavata (*ibid*, 35.30 ; Matsya, 113.28) and Ajanābha (Ind. Ant., 1899, p. 1).

7 Also called Hemakūṭa-varsha (Brahmāṇḍa, 34.44),

Harivarsha [1]—Bhārata being the southernmost region (varsha) separated from Kimpurusha by the Himavat chain, and described, like Uttara-kuru (the northernmost region), as being shaped like a bow.[2] To the seven original varshas [3] are added two others of a longitudinal character, *viz.*, Bhadrāśva (east of Meru) and Ketumāla (west of Meru), raising the number to nine.[4]

The description of the trans-Himālayan *Varshas* is, in the main, as idealistic and mythical as the account of the island continents

Haimavata-varsha (Mbh., vi. 6.7) and Kinnara-khaṇḍa (*Ain-i-Akbari*, iii, pp. 30.31).

[1] Also called Nishadha-varsha (*Brahmāṇḍa*, 34.45). The Garuḍa Purāṇa places Harivarsha in the South-West of Meru (Ch. 55.2).

[2] Dhanuḥ-saṁsthe cha vijñeye dve varshe dakshiṇ ottare (Matsya, 113.32 ; Brahmāṇḍa, 35.33 ; Mbh., vi 6.38).

[3] Sapta varshāṇi vakshyāmi Jambudvîpaṁ yathāvi dham (Matsya, 113-4). Varshāṇi yāni saptātra (Brahmāṇḍa 35.24) ; varshāṇi sapta (*ibid*, 28). *Cf.* Mbh., vi. 6.53.

[4] Nava Varshāṇi (Matsya, 114.85 ; Brahmāṇḍa. 34.48) ; navavarshaṁ Jambudvîpam (*ibid*, 35.7). *Cf.* Nīlakaṇṭha's Commentary on Mbh., vi. 6.37: "Kechid Bhadrāśva-Ketumālayor varshāntaratvaṁ prakalpya nava varshāṇîtyāchakshate."

The Brahmāṇḍa Purāṇa applies the names Mālyavad-varsha and Gandhamādana-varsha to Bhadrāśva and Ketumāla respectively (Ch. 34.47,48). In 45.24 and 46.35 Bhadrāśva is called Pūrvadvîpa (*cf.* Pūrva Videha). In Agni, 108.14, the name is given as Su-pārśva.

surrounding Jambudvîpa. The Mārkaṇḍeya Purāṇa naïvely says : [1]

yāni Kimpurushādyāni Varshāṇyashṭau dvijottama
teshūdbhidāditoyāni meghavāryatra Bhārate

* * * * *

na chaiteshu yugāvasthā nādhayo vyādhayo na cha
puṇyāpuṇya-samārambho naiva teshu dvijottama

"In Kimpurusha and the seven other countries, O Brāhman, waters bubble up *from the ground* ; here in Bhārata we have rain...And in these countries the ages do not exist, nor bodily nor mental sicknesses ; nor is there any undertaking involving merit or demerit there, O Brāhman" (Pargiter).

There are, however, some faint indications that the original accounts may have been based on some real knowledge of the topography and physical features of Central and perhaps also Northern Asia. The elevated *varsha* in the middle of Jambudvîpa may have reference to the high plateau between the Oxus and the Tarim valleys,

[1] Ch. 56. 12-26, *cf.* also Ch. 53.35,

yāni Kimpurushākhyāni varjjayitvā Himāhvayam,
teshāṁ svabhāvataḥ siddhiḥ sukhaprāyā hyayatnataḥ.

"Perfection *exists* naturally in Kimpurusha and the other *continents*, with the exception of that named from the mountain Hima; and the *perfection* is almost complete happiness *which comes* without exertion" (Pargiter).

not far from the sandy deserts of Central Asia—the Bālukārṇava which the Mahābhārata places close to Meru.[1] Ketumāla, the western Varsha, drained by the Vaṅkshu (Oxus),[2] which flows past "Chîna, Maru (desert), and the country of the Tushāras, Pahlavas, Daradas, Śakas,"[3] etc., is obviously to be connected with Western Turkestan, while Bhadrāśva watered by the Sîtā, the mythical prototype of the Yarkand and Yellow rivers,[4]

[1] Dr. Seal (*Vaishṇavism and Christianity*, 48-49) compares Mount Meru with "Pamir or Bam-i-duniya, the roof of the world." In the seventh century A. D. "the Po lo-se-na range of the great snow mountains" near the frontier of Kapis, was considered to be the highest mountain in Jambudvîpa (Watters, Yuan Chwang, ii. 267), and the Ts'ung Ling (Onion Range) the centre of that continent (*ibid*, pp. 270, 282). The Ts'ung Ling is the Bolor Tagh and Karakorum Mountains of modern geographers (Watters). It separates Eastern Turkestan from Western Turkestan.

[2] For Vakshu (Variants Chakshu, Sva-rakshu, Raṅkshu, Vaṅkshu), see Brahmāṇḍa, 51.47 ; Matsya, 121. 45 ; Mārk., Ch. 56.13 f.; 59.15, Ind. Ant., 1912, p. 265 f.

[3] Atha Chîna Marūṁschaiva
Taṅganān sarva -Mūlikān,
Sāndrāṁs Tushārāṁs Tampākān (Lampākān?)
Pahlavān Daradān Śakān,
etān Janapadān Chakshuḥ (=Vaṅkshu)
plāvayantî gatodadhim
(Vāyu, 47.44-45.)

[4] For Sîtā see Brahmāṇḍa, 45.17-24, 51. 44-45 and Vāyu, 41.43. The Brahmāṇḍa expressly connects this river

apparently stands for Eastern Turkestan and North China. Uttara-kuru placed beyond the Himālayas by the Aitareya Brāhmaṇa, and immediately to the south of *Uttaraḥ payasām nidhiḥ* (the Arctic Ocean) by the Rāmāyaṇa,[1] is an indefinite semi-mythic tract which Nabin Chandra Dās[2] identifies with certain countries in Northern Asia. Beyond this is the 'Northern deep'

> "Where springing from the billows high
> Mount Somagiri seeks the sky
> And lightens with perpetual glow
> The sunless realm that lies below.

Scholars find in these lines (sa tu deśo visūryo'pi tasya bhāsā prakāśate) a reference to the Aurora Borealis[3] and are inclined to credit the

with "Sirindhrān Kukurān Chînān," and also with the Rushas" (Russians?). The Matsya (121.43) has the reading "Saśailān Kukurān Randhrān Varvarān Yavanān Khasān" and the Vayu (47.43) "Sirindhrān Kuntalān Chinān Varvarān Yavanān Druhān." The Sîtā is apparently the Yarkand river (Watters, II. 283, 288).

According to one theory it flows underground until it emerges at the Chi-shih Mountain and becomes the source of the Yellow River of China (Watters, I. 32).

1 Kishkindhyā Kāṇḍa, Canto 43 (Bangabāsī edition).

2 A note on the Ancient Geography of Asia compiled from Vālmiki's Rāmāyaṇa, pp. 67.68.

3 Seal, *Vaishṇavism and Christianity* (MDCCCXCIX), p. 49.. The suggestion is already found in Nabin Chandra Dās's *Note on the Ancient Geography of Asia* (1896), pp. 67-68

Rāmāyaṇa with some accurate knowledge of the North. The Uttara-kuru of the Purāṇas is, however, a sort of El Dorado[1] which it would be futile to equate with any terrestrial region. Attempts have been made to identify the remaining trans-Himālayan Varshas[2] but without any plausibility.

Bhāratavarsha.

The southernmost *Varsha*, Bhārata, lying between the Himavat and the sea,[3] is, of course, India. The term, however, as used by Purāṇic cosmographers, embraces much more than India Proper as is apparent from the names of some of its divisions which "extend to the ocean, but are mutually

[1] *Cf.* Vāyu Purāṇa, 45. 1. 1 f. ; Pliny. Bk. XVI., c. 17 : "About the Attacori (Uttarakuru) Amometus composed a volume for private circulation similar to the work of Hecataeus about the Hyperboreans." (McCrindle, *Ancient India as described in Classical Literature*, p. 113 ; *cf.* also McCrindle, *Megasthenes and Arrian*, Chuckervertty and Chatterjee's ed., pp. 76-79.

[2] C. V. Vaidya, *Epic India*, p. 268 f.

Seal, *Vaishṇavism and Christianity*, pp. 47-50. The identification of Ramyaka with Rome is clearly untenable (*cf. Ain-i-Akbari*, iii. pp. 30-31).

[3] Uttaraṁ yat samudrasya Himavaddakshiṇaṇchayat
Varshaṁ tad Bhārataṁ nāma yatreyaṁ Bhāratī prajā
(Vāyu, 45.75-76).

Uttaraṁyat samudrasya Himādreśchaiva dakshiṇam
varshaṁtad Bhārataṁ nāma Bhāratī yatra santatiḥ
(Vishṇu, ii. 3.1).

inaccessible" (samudrāntaritā jñeyā ste tvagamyāḥ parasparam).[1] Among these are Kaṭāha [2] and Simhala, identified with Kedah [3] (in the Malay Peninsula) and Ceylon respectively.[4]

The name Bhāratavarsha is said to be derived from the legendary king Bharata [5] whom most of the Purāṇas represent as a descendant of Priyavrata, son of Manu Svāyambhuva.[6] We are told that Priyavrata had ten sons three of whom became recluses and the remaining seven were anointed as rulers of the seven great island continents of the Purāṇic world. Agnîdhra, who got Jambudvîpa, the innermost continent, had nine sons to each of whom he assigned the sovereignty of one of the nine *Varshas* into which his *dvîpa*

1 Mārk. P., 57.6.

2 Vāmana Pūraṇa, xiii. 10-11; Garuḍa, Ch. 55.5.

3 Sir Asutosh Mookerjee Silver Jubilee Volumes, Vol. III, Orientalia, Part I, pp. 3-4.

4 Alberuni (I, p. 295), says, "Bhāratavarsha is not India alone." Abul Fazl (Ain, III, p. 7) says, "Hindusthān is described as enclosed on the east, west and south by the ocean, but Ceylon, Achin, the Moluccas and a considerable number of islands are accounted within its extent." *Cf.* the reference to Yavadvîpa in the Rāmāyaṇa (iv. 40.30), Brahmāṇḍa (52. 14-19), and Vāyu (48.14 f.); (miscalled Yamadvîpa).

5 Himāhvam dakshiṇam Varsham Bharatāya nyavedayat.
tasmāt tad Bhāratam Varsham tasya nāmnā vidur budhāḥ (Brahmāṇḍa, 34.55).

6 Bhāgavata, xi. 2.15 f.

was divided.[1] Bhāratavarsha fell to the share of Nābhi. The son of Nābhi was Ṛishabha. And it was Bharata, son of Ṛishabha, who gave his name to the southern Varsha styled Himāhva.[3] In certain Purāṇic passages, however, it is stated that Bharata was an epithet of Manu himself and the country was named after him.[4] In view of the discrepant testimony of the Purāṇas it is perhaps not unreasonable to suggest that the name of the country south of the Himavat was derived, not from the mythical Bharata of the Purāṇas, but from the historical Bharata tribe (*cf.* Bhāratî prajā of *Vāyu,* 45,76 ; Bhāratî santatiḥ, *Vishṇu,* ii. 3. 1.) which plays so important a part in Vedic and Epic tradition. The political

[1] Garuḍa Purāṇa, Ch. 54; Brahmāṇda Purāṇa (Bangabāsi edition), Ch. 34.

[2] Nābhestu dakshiṇaṁ Varshaṁ Himāhvantu pitā dadau (Brahmāṇḍa, 34.44). *Cf.* the name Ajanābha given to Bhārata Varsha in the Bhāgavata Purāṇa (Ind. Ant., 1899, p. 1).

[3] The name Himāhva is derived from the Himālayan chain. *Cf.* also Brahmāṇḍa, Ch. 35.30, "idaṁ Haimavatam Varshaṁ Bhārataṁ nāma viśruta." In the Mahābhārata, however, (vi. 6,7) the name Haimavata is (also) applied to Kimpurusha-varsha.

[4] bharaṇāchcha prajānāṁ vai Manur Bharata uchyate
Nirukta-vachanāchchaiva Varshaṁ tat Bhārataṁ smṛitam.

(Matsya, 114.5 ; Brahmāṇḍa. 49.10). *Cf.* Alberuni (i. 251), "we find a tradition in the Vāyu Purāṇa that the

domination of the greater part of India by seven Bhāratas ' is testified to by Buddhist texts. The cultural supremacy of the tribe is equally clear from the evidence of the Ṛik and Yajus Saṁhitās, the Brāhmaṇas and the Great Epic which bears the name of *Mahābhārata*.

Foreign nomenclature of India.

While the Purāṇas name India after a mythical tree (Jambu), a legendary hero, or the great mountain of snow (Himạ) which walls it off from the rest of the world, foreigners, particularly those coming from the north-west, named it after the mighty river which, like the Nile in Egypt, constitutes the most imposing feature of that part of the country with which they first came into contact. It is only the Chinese pilgrims and Muslim scholars well-versed in Buddhist or Brāhmaṇical lore, who show acquaintance with the traditional Indian nomenclature, and employ terms suggestive of social and religious characteristics.

Of the names derived from the Sindhu (Persian Hindu, Greek Indus) the earliest are those recorded by the ancient Persians in the Avesta and the Inscriptions of Darius. In the Vendidad we have the name *Hapta Hindu*, doubtless identical with

centre (*sic*) of Jambudvîpa is called Bhāratavarsha, which means those who acquire something and nourish themselves."

Dialogues of the Buddha, Part II, p. 270.

Sapta Sindhavaḥ of the Ṛig Veda.[1] The famous name *Hi(n)du* occurs in the Persepolis and Naksh-i-Rustam inscriptions of Darius.[2] It corresponds to '*India*' of Herodotus which constituted the twentieth Satrapy of the Persian king and apparently signified only the Indus valley bounded on the east by the desert of Rājaputāna. "Of the Indians," says Herodotus, "the population is by far the greatest of all nations whom we know of, and they paid a tribute proportionately larger than all the rest, 360 talents of gold dust; this was the twentieth division. That part of India towards the rising sun is all sand...the Indians' country towards the east is a desert by reason of the sands."[3] But "India" was already acquiring a wider denotation, for Herodotus speaks of Indians who "are situated very far from the Persians, towards the south, and were never subject to Darius."[4]

In the days of Alexander and his immediate successors the term acquires a still wider meaning "in accordance with the law of geographical nomenclature."[5] Megasthenes, for instance, applies the name to the whole country "which is in shape quadrilateral," and has "its eastern as

1 Camb. Hist. Ind., Vol. I, p. 324.

2 *Ibid*, 335.

3 Book III, 97-98 (trans. by McCrindle).

4 *Ibid*, 101.

5 Rapson, *Ancient India*, p. 24.

well as its western side bounded by the great sea, but on the northern side it is divided by Mount Hemōdos from that part of Skythia which is inhabited by the Sakai, while the fourth or western side is bounded by the river called the Indus. The extent of the whole country from east to west is said to be 28,000 stadia, and from north to south 32,000."

A further stage in the widening of the denotation of India is reached in the days of Ptolemy who includes within its limits not only Hindusthān, but also the vast region lying beyond the Ganges (India extra Gangem).[1]

The earliest Chinese writers (*e.g.*, Chang-Kien and his successors) employ the terms Shên-tu and Hsien-tou (Sindhu) which is soon replaced by T'ien-chu.[2] With the Tang period came a new name Yin-tu which is soon confounded with Indu (the moon), and it is naïvely suggested that "the bright connected light of holy men and sages, guiding the world as the shining of the moon, have made this country eminent, and so it is called In-tu."[3]

Along with these foreign names of riparian origin and traditional Indian appellations like

[1] *Cf.* also Moreland, *India at the Death of Akbar*, 1-2.

[2] Watters, *Yuan Chwang*, i. 132, 137, 140.

[3] Beal, *Records* (Si-yu-ki), I, p. 69.

Jambudvîpa we find, in the records of Hiuen-Tsang and I-tsing, other designations of India which are suggestive of its geographical position in relation to China, its grand regional divisions, and its religious and social conditions, particularly the prominence of the Indra cult and the ascendency of the Aryans and especially of the Brāhmaṇas. Such names are Si-fang (the west), Wu-t'ien (the five countries of India), A-li-ya-t'i-sha (Āryadeśa), Po-lo-mên-kuo or Fan-kuo (Brahma-rāshṭra) and Indra-vardhana.[1]

The latest foreign name of India is probably Hindusthān which reminds us of ' Hi(n)du ' of the old Persian epigraphs. In Brāhmaṇical records the term Hindu is probably first met with in the inscriptions of the kings of Vijayanagara.[2] Like India, Hindusthān, too, had a wider and a narrower denotation. "Hindustān in its wider sense means all India lying north of the Vindhya mountains ; in the narrower sense, the upper basin of the Ganges. Further the term is sometimes loosely applied by modern writers to the whole of India."[3]

1 Takakusu, *I-tsing's Record*, p. lii. Watters, *Yuan Chwang*, i. 131-40.

2 *Cf.* Satyamaṅgalam plates, *Epigraphia Indica* iii. p. 38, " pararāja-bhayaṅkaraḥ Hiṁdurāya Suratrāṇo vaṁdivargeṇa varṇyate."

3 Roberts, *History of British India*, p. 2 n.

Shape of India according to the ancients.

In the description of Bhārata, as in the account of the "island" continent of which it constitutes the southernmost part, we have a curious blend of fact and fiction. This is apparent from the confusing and contradictory details about its shape and territorial divisions given in different sections of the Purāṇas. In some passages it is described quite correctly as being 'constituted with a fourfold conformation' (chatuḥ-saṁsthāna-saṁsthitam),[1] 'on its south and west and east is the great ocean, the Himavat range stretches along on its north like the string of a bow.' This accuracy is not, however, always maintained, and the Kūrma-niveśa section [2] shows a total misconception of the configuration of India by making it conform to the shape of a tortoise "lying outspread and facing eastwards." A third set of

[1] Mārk., 57.59. *Cf.* the description of India as a rhomboid, or unequa lquadrilateral by Eratosthenes and other writers (Cunn., *Geography*, 2; *Cambridge History of Ancient India*, Vol. I, pp. 400-402).

[2] Mārk. 58. *Cf.* also the Kūrma Vibhāga section of the Bṛihat Saṁhitā. In the Geography of Ptolemy, too, "the true shape of India is completely distorted, and its most striking feature, the acute angle formed by the meeting of the two coasts of the Peninsula at Cape Comorin is changed to a single coast line, running almost straight from the mouth of the Indus to the mouth of the Ganges" (Cunningham, *Ancient Geography of India*, ed., by, S. N. Majumdār Śāstrī, p. 9).

passages[1] describe India as being bow-like (*i.e.*, semi-circular) in shape thus ignoring the *triangular* form[2] of Peninsular India bounded by the sea.

The Nine Divisions of India.

The account of the nine-fold division (nava-bheda) of India shows the same mixture of inaccurate or imaginary details with sober statements of facts. In the *Nadyādi-varṇana* section (Canto 57) of the *Bhuvana-kosha* of the Mārkaṇḍeya Purāṇa for instance, we are told that Bhāratavarsha is cut up into nine parts (khaṇḍa or bheda) "which must be known as extending to the ocean, but as being mutually inaccessible."[3] They are—

Indradvîpaḥ Kaśerumāṁs Tāmraparṇo Gabhastimān
Nāgadvîpastathā Saumyo Gāndharvo Vāruṇastathā

[1] Dhanuḥsaṁsthe cha vijñeye dve varshe dakshiṇottare (Matsya, 113.32, Brahmāṇḍa, 35.33 ; Mbh., vi. 6.38). *Cf.* Nīlakaṇṭha, "Bhāratavarshasya dhanukākāratvam" (comm. on Mbh., vi. 6.3-5). Hiuen Tsang, too, apparently compares the shape of India to a half-moon, with the diameter or broad side to the north, and the narrow end to the south (Cunn., *Geography*, p. 12 ; Watters, *Yuan Chwang*, Vol. I, p. 140).

[2] Regarding the triangular shape of India see Nīlakaṇṭha's commentary on Mbh., vi. 6. 3-5—'Bhārata-varshastrikoṇaḥ,' and the Chinese Fah-kai-lip-to which says, " this country in shape is narrow towards the south, and broad towards the north (Cunn., *Geographg*, p. 12).

[3] Samudrāntaritā Jñeyāste tvagamyāḥ parasparam (Mārk., 575).

ayaṁ tu navamasteshāṁ dvîpaḥ sāgarasaṁvṛitaḥ[1]
yojanānāṁ sahasraṁ vai dvîpo'yaṁ dakshiṇottarāt
pūrve Kirātā yasyāste paśchime Yavanāstathā
Brāhmaṇāḥ Kshatriyāḥ Vaiśyāḥ Śūdrāśchāntaḥs-
thitā dvija.

The Vāmana Purāṇa[2] reads Kaṭāha and Siṁhala instead of Saumya and Gāndharva, and mentions Kumāra[3] (=Kumārikā,[4] Kaumārika-khaṇḍa) as the name of the *Navama dvîpa*. The ninth dvîpa having at its east end the land of the Kirātas[5] and

[1] Alberuni wrongly puts it as Nagarasaṁvṛitta (i. 295).

[2] xiii. 10-11 ; also Garuḍa, Ch. 55,5—Nāgadvīpaḥ Kaṭāhaścha Siṁhalo Vāruṇastathā.

[3] Kumārākhyaparikhyāto dvîpo'yaṁ dakshiṇottaraḥ (XIII. ii).

[4] Kumārikā Khaṇḍam, 39.69:
Indradvîpaḥ Kaśeruścha Tāmradvîpo Gabhastimān
Nāgaḥ Saumyaścha Gāndharvo Varuṇaścha Kumārikā
Rājaśekhara says in his *Kāvya Mīmāṁsā*, *Deśavibhāga* (p. 92) : tatredaṁ Bhārataṁ Varsham. Asya cha Nava bhedāḥ : Indradvîpaḥ...Kumārî dvîpaśchāyaṁ navamaḥ... atra cha Kumārî-dvîpe
Vindhyaścha Pāripātraścha Suktimān Ṛikshaparvataḥ
Mahendra-Sahya-Malayāḥ saptaite Kulaparvatāḥ
Cf. also the 'Kumāra Khaṇḍa' of the *Ain-i-Akbari*, iii. p. 31.

[5] Doubtless identical with the Kirrhadia of Ptolemy (ed. S. N. Majumdār, p. 219), located near Mount Maiandros. For the position of Mount Mahendra in relation to Kumārîdvîpa and Indradvîpa, see Skanda Purāṇa, Kumārikā Khaṇḍa, 39.113.

at the west the Yavanas,[1] and inhabited by the Brāhmaṇas, Kshatriyas, Vaiśyas and Śūdras, is obviously India proper,[2] here regarded as only a *part* of Bhārata-varsha which must, therefore, be taken to denote a wider area. The epithet "sāgarasaṁvṛitaḥ" applied to Kumârî Dvîpa hardly accords with reality because India proper "is not surrounded by the sea, but bounded by it only on the east, south, and west, and only partially so in the east and west for verse 8 places the

[1] *Cf.* the Yonas mentioned in the inscriptions of Aśoka in connection with the Kambojas and Gandhāras, and the country of the Yonas referred to in the Mahāvaṁsa (Geiger's trans., p. 85). Their capital was Alasanda (=Alexandria, Geiger, p. 194 n) near Kābul.

[2] *Cf.* the Matsya (114-10) and Brahmāṇḍa passage (49.15): "āyato hyā Kumārikyādā Gaṅgā-prabhavāchcha vai." The Skanda Purāṇa restricts 'Kaumārika Khaṇḍa' to the territory between the Pāriyātra and Mahendra (Kumārikā Khaṇḍa, 39.113), while according to the Garuḍa Purāṇa (Ch. 55.6) it was bounded on the east by the Kirātas, on the west by the Yavanas, on the south by the Andhras and on the north by the Turushkas:—

pūrve Kirātā stasyāste paśchime Yavanāḥ sthitāḥ
Andhrā dakshiṇato Rudra, Turushkāstvapi chottare

The Kumārī dvîpa, according to the Mārkaṇḍeya passage quoted above is "a thousand yojanas from south to north." Patrokles put down the distance as 15,000 stades (1,724 miles, Camb. Hist., p. 400). Megasthenes put the extent at 22,300 stades. The actual distance is about 1,800 miles. The distance from west to east, where it is shortest is about 1,360 miles (Camb. Hist.).

Kirātas and Yavanas there respectively."[1] It is not easy to say how many of the other dvîpas belong to the domain of sober geography, and our task is rendered more difficult by the obvious corruption of the text as is evidenced by the substitution, in most of the Purāṇas, of Saumya and Gāndharva in place of the well-known lands of Kaṭāha and Siṁhala.[2]

Alberuni with singular inaccuracy represents Indradvîpa as identical with Mid-India.[3] Abul Fazl shows greater acquaintance with Purāṇic tradition by placing it between Laṅkā and Mahendra.[4] In the Skanda Purāṇa Indradvîpa is expressly mentioned as lying beyond the Mahendra range.[5] If the testimony of the *Ain-i-Akbari* and the Skanda Purāṇa is to be accepted we shall have to place Indradvîpa somewhere beyond the Mahendra (Eastern Ghāṭs), *i.e.*, in the Bay of Bengal. But where is the 'island' in the Bay of Bengal which answers to the Purāṇic description of Indradvîpa? The ingenious suggestion of

1 Pargiter, Mārkaṇḍeya P., p. 284 n.

2 Only the Vāmana and Garuḍa Purāṇas retain the names of Kaṭāha and Siṁhala.

3 'Indradvîpa' or Madhyadeśa, *i.e.*, the middle country (Vol. I, p. 296).

4 *Ain-i-Akbari*, iii. p. 31.

5 Mahendraparataśchaiva Indradvîpo nigadyate
Pāriyātrasya chaivārvāk Khaṇḍaṁ Kaumārikaṁ
smṛitam
(Skānda, Kumārikā-khaṇḍa, 39.113.)

Mr. S. N. Majumdār Śāstrî that Indradvîpa is Burma deserves attention and may explain why Ptolemy was led to place Maiandros (Mahendra) in India extra Gangem.

Kaśerumat is placed by Alberuni to the east of the Madhyadeśa, and by Abul Fazl between Mahendra and Śukti. Mr. Majumdār's identification with the Malaya Peninsula lacks plausibility.[1]

Tāmravarṇa (Tāmraparṇa according to the Kūrma and Tāmraparṇî according to the Matsya Purāṇa) is usually identified with Ceylon which the ancient Greeks called Taprobane, and Aśoka refers to as Taṁbapaṁni. But this identification is hardly tenable in view of the fact that the Garuḍa Purāṇa clearly distinguishes it from Siṁhala. Alberuni places it in the south-east of India, and Abul Fazl identifies it with the tract between Śukti and Malaya. These facts probably point to the district drained by the river Tāmraparṇî which rises in the Malaya range. But this view can hardly be reconciled with the statement in the Kāvya-mîmāṁsā that all the Kula-parvatas, including the Malaya, were in the Kumārîdvîpa,

[1] In the Mahābhārata, iii. 12.32, Kaserumat is the name of a Yavana chief killed by Krishṇa—Indradyumno hataḥ kopād Yavanaścha Kaserumān. The Sabhāparva (31.72) mentions a Yavanānāṁ puram not far from the sea-coast, from which envoys are said to have been sent to Vibhîshaṇa, king of Laṅkā.

which is sharply distinguished from Tāmravarṇa. Equally unacceptable is the view of Abul Fazl that Gabhastimat lies between the Ṛiksha and the Malaya, and the Nāgadvîpa between the Ṛiksha and the Pāriyātra. Alberuni places the former south of the Madhyadeśa and the latter on the south-west. Nāgadvîpa may refer to the Jaffna peninsula which Tamil tradition represents as the domain of a Nāga king.[1]

Saumya obviously is a misreading for Kaṭāha, identified by Çoedes, a French scholar, with the present port of Kedah in the Malay Peninsula.[2]

'Gāndharva', placed by Alberuni on the north-west of the Madhyadeśa, may stand for Gandhāra as a passage of the Rāmāyaṇa seems to suggest.[3] But it can hardly be characterised as a 'dvîpa' inaccessible from India proper. The reading 'Siṁhala' found in the Garuḍa Purāṇa seems to be preferable. 'Siṁhala' is of course Ceylon or a part of it.

Vāruṇa, the eighth division of Bhārata, is omitted by Alberuni. Abul Fazl identifies it with the western portion of the tract between the Sahya (the Western Ghāṭs) and the Vindhya.

[1] Smith, EHI, 4th edition, p. 491. *cf. Mahāvaṁsa* (translated by Geiger), p. 6. Tāmraparṇa, Nāgadvîpa and Siṁhala may refer to distinct *parts* of Ceylon.

[2] Sir Asutosh Mookerjee Silver Jubilee Volumes, Vol. III, Orientalia, Part I, p. 4.

[3] Uttarakāṇḍa, 113.11; 114.11.

While the description of Bhārata by the Purāṇic cosmographers as an aggregate of nine islands which are mutually inaccessible can hardly be made to accord with reality, the ninefold division (nava-bheda) of astrologers set forth in the Kūrma-niveśa section is of a different character.[1] Though there is even here considerable misconception in regard to the assignment of the various *janapadas* to particular divisions, due in part to the absurd attempt to make the shape of India conform to that of a tortoise (Kūrma) lying out-spread and facing eastwards, the divisions themselves are of a geographical character being based on the points of the compass.

The most accurate account, however, from the purely geographical point of view, of the main

[1] The nava-bheda of astrologers is best described in the following words of Alberuni (Sachau, I,pp. 296-298) :—

"Astronomers and astrologers divide the directions according to the lunar stations. Therefore the country, too, is divided according to the lunar stations, and the figure which represents this division is similar to a tortoise. Therefore it is called Kūrma-chakra, *i.e.*, the tortoise circle or the tortoise shape. The following diagram is from the Saṁhitā of Varāhamihira.

Varāha calls each of the nava-khaṇḍa a Varga. He says : 'By them (the Vargas) Bhāratavarsha is divided into nine parts, the central one, the eastern, etc.' Another astronomer who described the nava-khaṇḍa is Parāśara. The Purāṇic compilers apparently borrowed the Kūrma-niveśa section from astronomical works.

territorial divisions of India, is that contained in the verses of the Nadyādi-varṇana section which describe the seven regions of 'Kumārî Dvipa,'[1]

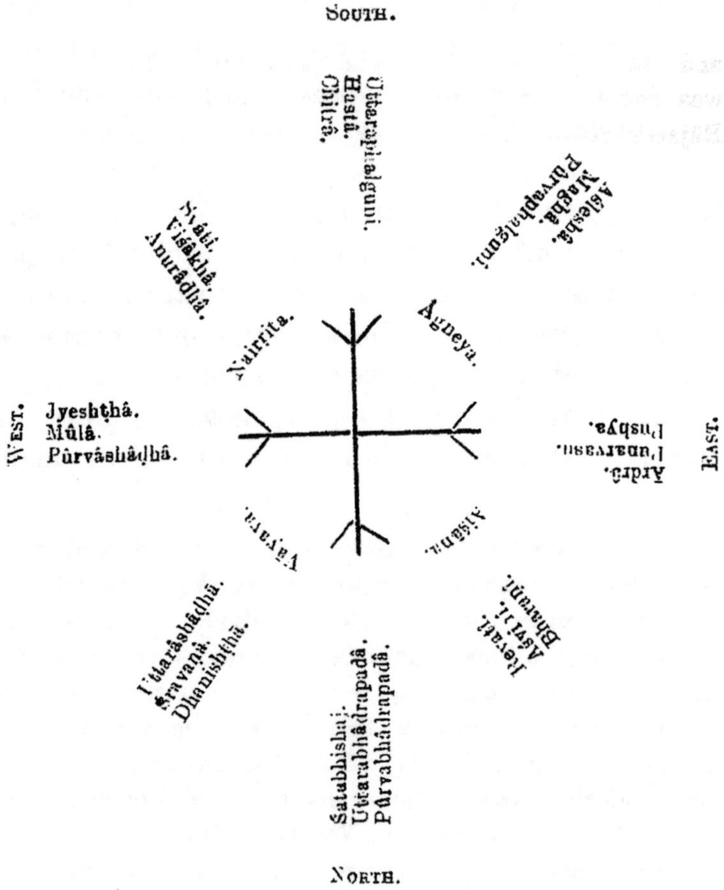

[1] *Cf.* tairidaṁ Bhāratam Varshaṁ saptakhaṇḍaṁ kṛitaṁ purā (Brahmāṇḍa, 34.64).

The primary division was into five great regions which are already met with in the Atharva Veda (xix. 17.1-9) *viz.*, the Madhyadeśa, Udîchya, Prāchya, Dakshiṇāpatha, Aparānta, the Vindhyan region, and the 'Parvatāśrayin' or Himālayan region.

and the Aitareya Brāhmaṇa (viii. 14). This division was adopted by Buddhist writers and authors like Rājaśekhara.

CHAPTER VII

The Mountain System of the Purāṇas

The entire mountain system of the world, as conceived by Purāṇic writers, centres round Meru which is supposed to stand in the middle of Ilâvṛita, the most centrally situated and highly elevated sub-continental region (*varsha*) of Jambudvîpa, the innermost of the great island continents of the world, which is said to be surrounded on all sides by the sea of salt.[1] The terraqueous globe, as is well-known, is described by ancient Hindu cosmographers as comprising seven concentric islands (*Saptadvîpa Vasundharā*)[2] separated by encircling seas which are likewise seven in number. The innermost of these *dvîpas* is Jambudvîpa. It is described as low on the south and north, and highly elevated in the middle.[3] On the southern half of the elevated ground are three sub-continents (*varsha*), *viz.*, Bhārata, Kimpurusha and Harivarsha. On the north, too, are three, *viz.*, Ramyaka, Hiraṇmaya and Uttara

[1] Agni Purāṇa, Chs. 107-108 ; Mārkaṇḍeya Purāṇa, Ch. 54, Pargiter's trans., p. 275 f.

[2] Saptadvîpā Vasumatî (Patañjali's Mahābhāshya, Kielhorn's edition, i. 9).

[3] Dakshiṇottarato nimnā madhye tuṅgāyatā kshitiḥ (Mārk. P., 54. 12).

Kuru. Ilâvṛita is situated between those halves, and is said to be shaped like the half moon. East of it is Bhadrāśva and west is Ketumâla. Meru, "the mountain of gold," stands in the middle of Ilâvṛita.

Below the central mountain are, we are told the four *Vishkambha Parvatas* ("subjacent hills") :—Mandara on the east, Gandhamādana on the south, Vipula on the west and Supārśva on the north.

Each of the northern and southern *varshas* has its own sub-continental range (*varsha-parvata*). Three of the varsha-parvatas, *viz.*, Nîla, the parvata of Ramyaka, Śveta (or Śukla), the parvata of Hiraṇmaya or Śvetavarsha,[1] and Śṛiṅgî (Śṛiṅgavat or Tri śṛiṅga),[2] the parvata of Uttara-kuru,[3] lie to the north of Meru. Three others, *viz.*, Nishadha, the parvata of Harivarsha,

[1] Agni P., 107. 7. Śveta Varsha is apparently the Śveta Dvîpa of the Nārāyaṇîya story. Mbh., vi. 8, associates Śveta with 'Ramaṇaka,' and Nîla with Hiraṇmaya, *cf.* also Seal, *Vaishṇavism*, p. 47 f.

[2] Mārk. p. 54. 9; Mbh., VI. 6. 4 ff. ; Agni, 108. 26.

[3] Airāvata-varsha according to the Mbh., vi. 6. 37; 8. 11. The Mahābhārata places Uttara-kuru to the south of Nîla and on the border of Meru (Mbh., vi. 7. 2). Referring to the northernmost region the Great Epic says "na tatra Sūryastapati." The Rāmāyaṇa also tells us (iv. 43. 55) "sa tu deśo visūryopi tasya bhāsā prakāśate." N. Dās and Seal find here a reference to the Aurora Borealis.

Hemakūṭa, the parvata of Kimpurusha-varsha and Himavat, the parvata of Bhārata, Himāhvaya or Haimavata-varsha [1] lie to its south.[2] These Varsha-parvatas seem to be conceived as parallel ranges stretching east and west and extending into the ocean.[3] Their number is stated to be six. But the inclusion of Meru, the mountain of the central Varsha, raises the total number to seven.[4]

In addition to the Varsha-parvatas which mark off the northern, central and southern varshas from each other and, in some cases, actually give the sub-continents their distinctive names, [5] every *varsha* has seven principal ranges

[1] Agni P., 107. 5; Brahmāṇḍa, 35. 30. In Mbh., vi. 6. 7, the name Haimavata is given to the Kimpurusha-varsha, the Kinnarakhaṇḍa of Abul Fazal, *Ain-i-Akbari*, Trans., iii. 30-31, and of Shāhu Chhatrapati.

[2] Agni P., 107. 5-7 ; 10. 8. 5.

[3] Samudrāntaḥ pravishṭāścha saḍasmin Varshaparvatāḥ (Mārk. P., 54. 12).

Prāgāyatā suparvāṇaḥ saḍime Varshaparvatāḥ.
avagāḍhāḥ ubhayataḥ samudrau pūrvapaśchimau
—Brahmāṇḍa, 35. 13; Padma, Svarga, 2. 22;
Mbh., vi. 6. 3.

[4] Himavān Hemakūṭaścha Ṛishabho (variant Nishadho) Merureva cha.

Nīlah Svetas tathā Sriṅgî saptāsmin Varshaparvatāḥ
(Mārk. P., 54. 9).

[5] *Cf.* the names Meruvarsha (Mārk., 59), Svetavarsha (Agni, 107), and Haimavata-varsha (Brahmāṇḍa. 35).

styled *Kula-parvata*[1] (group-mountain or clan-mountain), besides a number of smaller hills (kshudra-parvatāḥ)[2] which are situated near these (bhūdharāḥ ye samîpagāḥ). The names of the Kula-parvatas of Bhārata-varsha are thus given in the Great Epic and the Purāṇas :—

Mahendro Malayaḥ Sahyaḥ
Suktimān Ṛiksha-parvataḥ
Vindhyaścha Pāripātraścha
saptaivātra Kulāchalāḥ.[3]

The four outlying sub-continents, *viz.*, Bhadrāśva, Ketumāla, Bhārata and Uttara-Kuru are marked off from Ilāvṛita and other inner varṣhas by a group of ranges styled *Maryādā-parvatas* (boundary mountains).[4] These are eight in number, *viz.*, Jaṭhara and Devakūṭa on the east side of Meru, separating the central *varsha* (Ilāvṛita) from Bhadrāśva;[5] Nishadha (No. 2) and Pāripātra

1 Sarveshveteshu Varsheshu sapta sapta Kulāchalāḥ. —Agni. 108. 32. According to the Mārk. P., Bhadrāśva has five Kulāchalas. But Ketumāla, like Bhārata, has seven (Ch. 59). According to Hopkins (*Epic Mythology*, 9n) " The Seven Mountains, known as doors of heaven. appear in Vedic literature (TS. 3, 12. 2, 9 ; 6, 2, 4, 3)."

2 Mārk. 59. 5.

3 Mbh. vi. 9.11, Mārk. 57.10.

4 Bhāratāḥ Ketumālāścha Bhadrāśvāḥ Kuravastathā patrāṇi lokapadmasya Maryādāśaila-bāhyataḥ. (Agni, 108.22.23.)

5 Mārk. 54. 22-26 ; 59. 3.4.

(No. 2) on the west, separating Ilāvṛita from Ketumāla ; Kailāsa and Himavat on the south marking off Bhārata from the central Varshas ; Śṛiṅgavat and Jārudhi (or Rudhira)[1] on the north cutting off Uttara-Kuru from the rest of Jambudvîpa.

The distinction between the Maryādā-parvatas and the Varsha-parvatas is not easily understood, and some of the former, notably Himavat and Śṛiṅgavat (=Śṛiṅgî) actually figure as Varsha-parvatas. It is, however, to be noted that the name Maryādā-parvata is given to mountains on *all* sides of Meru which separate the central varsha or varshas from the four outermost sub-continents. Varsha-parvatas, on the other hand, include Meru itself and the ranges separating the northern and southern (but not the eastern and western) [2] varshas from one another. All of them, with the exception of Meru, are represented as running from east to west and extending to the sea. That there is overlapping in regard to the northernmost and southernmost ranges is what may naturally be expected. The innermost Varsha-parvatas, *viz.*,

[1] Agni, 108.26.

[2] The number of Varshas seems to have been originally seven (sapta Varshāṇi, Mbh. vi. 6-53). The inclusion of Bhadrāśva and Ketumāla afterwards raised the number to nine. *Cf.* Nīlakaṇṭha "atraiva kechid Bhadrāśva-Ketumālayor varshāntaratvam prakalpya Navavarshāṇ-ityāchakshate."

Nîla and Nishadha, lying immediately to the north and south of Meru, join two other ranges, *viz.*, the Mālyavat and Gandhamādana (No. 2) which are associated with the eastern and western Maryādā-parvatas respectively, and completely shut off Ilāvṛita from the rest of the world.[1] They are the *Quadrangular mountains* referred to by Alberuni.[2]

There is much that is fabulous in the Purāṇic account summarised above. The division of the globe into seven concentric islands is, of course, entirely imaginary, though some of these *dvîpas* refer to real countries inhabited by historic peoples.[3] The description of the earth as low on the south and north, and highly elevated in the middle, and the account of the Varsha-parvatas and the Maryādā-parvatas given above, may, on the other hand, have been based upon stories recounted by travellers and traders, pilgrims and

1 *Ain-i-Akbari*, iii, pp. 30-31. *Cf.* Mārk. 54. 22-23.

2 "In the east the Mālyavant (parallel to Jaṭhara and Devakūṭa ?), in the north Ānila (*sic*), in the west the Gandhamādana (parallel to Nishadha No. 2, and Pāripātra ?), and in the south the Nishadha (No. 1).—Alberuni, i. 248. *Cf.* Mbh. vi. 6.9; Brahmāṇḍa Purāṇa, Ch. 45.

3 Śākadvîpa, for example, undoubtedly refers to a part of Irān (Seistān ?). The Brahma Purāṇa (Ch. 20. 71 f.) and the Agni Purāṇa (119, Ch. 21) refer to the Maga Brāhmaṇas who inhabit the Dvîpa and worship *Sūrya-rūpa-dharo Hariḥ*. Kuśadvîpa may refer to the country of the Kushāns.

explorers, about the orographical features of Middle Asia—the great plateau in its centre, and the hills and mountains which intersect it, marking off the tablelands from one another and from the level plains watered by the Ganges, the Oxus (Vaṁkshu)[1] and other streams. But the details, as given in the Purāṇas, are too fantastic and conventional to accord with reality ; and there is reason to believe that some of the so-called Varshaparvatas were in fact parts of the Himālayan chain which poetic fancy transformed into mounts of gold and classed as independent and parallel ranges haunted by supernatural beings who enjoyed eternal felicity.[2] Alberuni, for example, tells us that Meru is in Himavat and cites the authority of Āryabhaṭa in support of this view.[3] He further informs us that Mount Nishadha is close to the pond Vishṇupada whence

[1] Ketumālamato Varshaṁ nibodha mama paśchimaṁ............

ye pibanti mahānadyo Raṁkshuṁ (Vaṁkshuṁ) Syāmāṁ Sakambalām (Mārk. 59. 12-15).

[2] *Cf.* Ilāvṛitasya madhye tu Meruḥ Kanakaparvataḥ.—Mārk. 54. 14 ; Brahmāṇḍa, 35.15f. ; 44.2f. ; Agni, 107.9f. ; Alberuni, i.147 ; Mbh. vi. 6.10 f. The association of Meru with the " Bālukārṇava " to the north of the Himavat (Mbh. xvii. 1-2) suggests that the Purāṇic writers understood by Ilāvṛita a region not far from the desert of Gobi. *Cf.* also " Poh-lu-ka " of Yuan Chwang (I, p. 64 f.).

[3] Alberuni, i. 246.

comes the river Sarasvatī.[1] The contiguity of Nishadha to the source of the Sarasvati leaves no room for doubt that it, too, must have really been connected with the Himālayan chain. According to Pargiter, Hemakūṭa was "a mountain or group of mountains in the Himālayas in the western part of Nepal."[2] Thus many of the so-called Varsha-parvatas merge in the Himavat range which is the one great mountain chain connected with the plateau of Central Asia about which we have some authentic details in our ancient literature.

The oldest designation of the range is Himavat —the Imaos of classical writers. The current name Himālaya is first met with in the Bhagavad-Gītā and the works of Kālidāsa, though some scholars equate it with 'Sîmalia,' queen of the snow mountains, known to the ancient Babylonians.[3]

The **Himavat** had a wider denotation in ancient times. This is made clear by all our ancient authorities, Indian as well as Greek. A passage of the Mārkaṇḍeya Purāṇa says—" such is this country Bhārata, constituted with a fourfold conformation. On its south and west and east is the great ocean, the Himavat range stretches along

[1] Alberuni, ii, 142.

[2] Mārk. P., p. 360. Kailāsa, too, stands *Himavataḥ pṛishṭhe* (Matsya, 121.2).

[3] *Cambridge History of India,* Vol. I, p. 76.

on its north, like the string of a bow." [1] Referring to this passage Pargiter observes, "this implies that the Himavat range included also the Sulaiman Mountains along the west of the Pañjāb. The simile must refer to a drawn bow, with the string angular in the middle." That the Himavat included the Sulaiman range is also proved by those passages which say that it stretched from the eastern to the western ocean, and that the city of Pushkarāvatî (in the Peshāwār District) adorned it like a garland.[2] The classical writers, too,

[1] etattu Bhāratam Varshaṁ chatuḥ saṁsthāna-saṁsthitam.
dakshiṇāparato hyasya pūrveṇa cha mahodadhiḥ,
Himavānuttareṇāsya kārmukasya yathā guṇaḥ.
(Mārk. 57.59.)

[2] Avagāḍhā hyubhayataḥ Samudrau pūrvapaśchimau.
(Mbh. vi. 6.3.)
Kailāso Himavāṁśchaiva dakshiṇena mahābalau
pūrva-paśchāyatāvetāvarṇavāntar vyavasthitau.
(Mārk. P. 54.24.)
astyuttarasyāṁ diśi devatātmā
Himālayo nāma nagādhirājaḥ
pūrvāparau toyanidhî vagāhya
sthitaḥ prithivyā iva mānadaṇḍaḥ.
(Kumāra-sambhava, i. 1.)
Maulimālāṁ Himagirer nagarîṁ Pushkarāvatîm.
(Kathā-sarit-sāgara, 37.82.)
asti Prāleya-śailāgre nagarî Pushkarāvatî (*Ibid*, 37.22).
niśîthe cha Himādrau tāmanurāgaparā pituḥ
purîṁ Vidyādharapateḥ prāptavān Pushkarāvatîm.
(*Ibid*, 37.180.)

describe the Imaos as the source not only of the Indus and the Ganges, but also of the Koa (Kābul river) and the Souastos (Swāt).[1] This leaves no room for doubt that the western part of the range embraced the contiguous hills of Kābulistān.

The intimate acquaintance of the ancient Hindu writers with the Himavat is proved by frequent references to peaks like the Mūjavat or Muñjavat,[2] Tri-kakud (or Tri-kakubh)[3] and Saurya.[4] From Mūjavat came the famous plant, Soma, and from Tri-kakud came the salve Āñjana. Parts of the great chain remained, however, unexplored, and the deficiency of knowledge was made up by legends about Mahā Meru, Maināga, Krauñcha and Manoravasarpaṇa which we come across already in the later Vedic period.[5]

As already stated, Bhārata, like other Varshas, is described in the Purāṇas as being adorned by a number of comparatively small ranges, besides

[1] Ptolemy, vii. 1.26 (Majumdār's ed., p. 81).

[2] See *Vedic Index* and Mbh. xiv. 8.1.

[3] *Vedic Index* ; Matsya, 121.15. *Cf.* the three-peaked sacred mountain, about 20 miles north of Jammu, mentioned by Carmichael Smyth (*A History of the Reigning Family of Lahore*, 252 ; Prinsep, *Origin of the Sikh Power*, Ch. 8).

[4] Patañjali's *Mahābhāshya*, Kielhorn's ed., I, p. 150: Saurye nāma Himavataḥ śriṅge.'

[5] The first three are mentioned in the Taittirîya Āraṇyaka and the last one in the Satapatha Brāhmaṇa. See the *Vedic Index*. *Cf.* Brahmāṇḍa Purāṇa, 43.27 f.

the mighty Varsha-parvata on its north. These are styled **Kulāchalas** or **Kula-parvatas**. In the account of these mountains we reach the *terra firma* of solid facts. The Kula-parvatas are seven in number, *viz.*, Mahendra, Malaya, Sahya, Suktimān, Ṛiksha, Vindhya and Pāripātra or Pāriyātra. They are placed by Rājaśekhara in that part of Bhārata-varsha which was known as Kumārî Dvîpa.[1]

The meaning of the word 'Kula-parvata' or 'Kulāchala' is not explained in the Bhuvana-kosha or geographical section of the Purāṇas. Some such group of mountains must have been known to Ptolemy who speaks of the Apokopa, Sardonyx, Ouïndion, Bettigo, Adeisathron, Ouxenton, Oroudian, Bepyrrhos, Maiandros, Damassa and Semanthinos ranges.[2] Ouïndion, Adeisathron, Ouxenton and Maiandros clearly sound like

1 Kāvya Mîmāṁsā, Deśavibhāga: "Tatredaṁ Bhāratam Varsham. Asya cha navabhedāḥ......Kumārî Dvîpaśchāyaṁ navamaḥ.......Atra cha Kumārî-dvîpe

Vindhyaścha Pāripātraścha Suktimān Ṛiksha-parvataḥ
Mahendra-Sahya-Malayāḥ saptaite Kula-parvatāḥ
(p. 92).

2 Ptolemy, VII. i. 19-25; ii. 8. Apokopa has been identified by scholars with the Aravalli mountains, Sardonyx with Sātpurā, Ouïndion with Vindhya, Bettigo with Malaya (Tamil Podigai), Adeisathron with the Western Ghāṭs in which the Kāverî rises, Ouxenton with the Ṛiksha, Oroudian with the Vaidūrya (northern section of the Western Ghāṭs), Bepyrrhos (Vipula?) and Damassa

Vindhya, Sahyādri, Ṛikshavat and Mahendra respectively, though by strange errors of information the Western geographer was made to misplace most of them, notably the Mahendra range, which, along with Tosali and Triliṅga, is located in India *extra Gangem*. Bettigo is, as we shall see later on, the Greek equivalent of Po digai, the Tamil name of the Malaya. It is thus clear that Ptolemy knew most, if not all, of the Kula-parvatas. But the distinctive nomenclature of the group is not found in his work. It is, however, constantly met with in the epic and the post-epical literature of the Hindus, and is apparently hinted at by that acute foreign observer, Alberuni, who speaks of the "great knots" of Mount Meru, *viz.*, Mahendra, Malaya, etc.[1]

The word *Kula*, has the meaning of race, country or tribe.[2] And it is significant that each Kula-parvata is particularly associated with a distinct country or tribe. Thus Mahendra is the mountain *par excellence* of the Kaliṅgas,[3] Malaya

with the Eastern Himālayas, Maiandros with the Yuma chain of Arakan, and Semanthinos with the "extreme limit of the world" (S. N. Majumdār's Ptolomy, pp. 70-81, 204-207).

[1] Alberuni, Ch. 23 (p. 247); Ch. 25 (p. 257).

[2] See Āpte's Dictionary.

[3] *Cf.* Raghuvaṁśa, vi. 53-54, where the king of Kaliṅga is called "Asau Mahendrādrisamānasāraḥ patir Mahendrasya mahodadheścha," *cf.* also the Chicacole grants of Indravarman (*Ind. Ant.*, xiii. 120-123).

of the Pāṇḍyas,[1] Sahya of the Aparāntas,[2] Śuktimat of the people of Bhallāṭa,[3] Ṛiksha of the people of Māhishmatî,[4] Vindhya of the Āṭavyas and other forest folk of central India,[5] and Pāripātra or Pāriyātra of the Nishādas.[6]

Mahendra is frequently mentioned in literature and inscriptions. On it stood the hermitage of Rāma (Jāmadagnya).[7] It is said to have been conquered by epic heroes like Raghu [8] and also historical kings like Gautamîputra [9] Śātakarṇi

1 *Cf.* the epithets ' Malaya-dhvaja ' and ' Podiya-verpan ' given to the Pāṇḍya king in the Mahābhārata (viii. 20. 20, 21) and Tamil literature (Hultzsch in *Ind. Ant.*, 1889, 204 f.) respectively.

2 *Cf.* Raghuvaṁśa, iv. 52-59.

3 Bhallāṭamabhito jigye Śuktimantaṁ cha parvatam (Mbh. ii. 30. 5 f.).

4 Mahāśmasaṅghātavatî Ṛikshavantam upāśritā
Māhiśmatî nāma purî prakāśamupayāsyati
(Harivaṁśa, Vishṇuparva, 38. 19).

5 Āṭavyāḥ Śavarāścha ye
Pulindā Vindhya-Mauleyā Vaidarbhā Daṇḍakaiḥ-saha.
(Matsya, 114. 46-48, Vāyu, 45.126; Mārk. 57. 47, etc.)

6 Kāyavyo nāma Naishādiḥ......Pāriyātracharaḥ sadā (Mbh. xii. 135. 3-5).

7 Mahendrādrau Rāmaṁ dṛishṭvābhivādya cha (Bhāgavata, x. 79).

8 Śriyam Mahendranāthasya jahāra na tu medinîm (Raghu. iv. 48).

9 Rapson, *Andhra Coins*, p. xxxiv.

and Samudra Gupta.[1] It is said to have formed the southern boundary of the empire which Yaśodharman claims to have subdued.[2] On its "pure summit" was established the holy Gokarṇa-svāmî whose feet were worshipped by Indravarman and other kings of Kaliṅga-nagara.[3] Pargiter [4] identifies the Mahendra range with the portion of the Eastern Ghāṭs between the Godāvarî and the Mahānadî rivers, part of which near Ganjam, as pointed out by Wilson,[5] is still called Mahindra Malei or hills of Mahindra. The restriction of the name Mahendra to the *ghāṭs* on the north of the Godāvarî, seems to be supported by (*a*) the intimate association of the range with the Kaliṅga country, (*b*) the names of the rivers issuing from it—the Ṛishikulyā (which flows past Ganjam), the Vaṁśadharā (which has Kaliṅgapatam on its banks) and the Lāṅgulinî or Lāṅgulîya (on which stands Chicacole),[6] and (*c*) the lines of the Bhāgavata Purāṇa which clearly place Mahendrādri between

1 Fleet, *Corpus*, III, p. 7.

2 Ā-Lauhity-opakaṇṭhāt tāla-vana-gahan-opatyakādā-Māhendrāt (*ibid*, 146).

3 *Ind. Ant.*, xiii, 120 f.

4 Mārk. P. 284.

5 Vishṇu, II, iii n.

6 Mārk. P., Ch. 57.

'Gangā-sāgara-saṅgama' and 'Sapta-Godāvarî.'

But the restriction suggested by these lines is not always observed by our ancient writers as the following passages of the Rāmāyaṇa would seem to indicate :—

yuktaṁ kapāṭaṁ Pāṇḍyānāṁ gatā drakshyatha vānarāḥ
tataḥ samudramāsādya sampradhāryārtha-niśchayam
Agastyenāntare tatra sāgare viniveśitaḥ
chitrasānur-nagaḥ śrîmān Mahendraḥ parvatot-tamaḥ
jātarūpamayaḥ śrîmānavagāḍho mahārṇavam.
(Kishk. 41. 18-20.)

taṁ Sahyaṁ samatikramya Malayañcha mahāgirim
Mahendramatha samprāpya Rāmo rājîvalochanaḥ
āruroha mahābāhuḥ śikharaṁ drumabhūshitam
tataḥ śikharamāruhya Rāmo Daśarathātmajaḥ
kūrma-mîna-samākîrṇam apaśyat salilāśayam
āsedurānupūrvyeṇa samudraṁ bhîmaniḥsvanam.
(Laṅkā, 4. 92-94.)

In the Sundara Kāṇḍa "Mount Mahendra is said to have the foam of the sea collected about it,

[1] Gayāṁ gatvā pitṛînishṭvā Gaṅgā-sāgara-saṅgame
upaspṛiśya Mahendrādrau Rāmaṁ dṛishṭvābhivādya cha
Sapta Godāvarîṁ Venvāṁ Pampāṁ Bhîmarathîṁ tataḥ
(Bhāg. P., x. 79).

though Velāvana may have intervened between it and the sea." [1] Pargiter regards the Mahendra of the Rāmāyaṇa as altogether distinct from Mahendra of the Purāṇas, and identifies the former with the most southerly spur of the Travancore hills. There is actually in the Tinnevelly District a mountain called Mahendragiri [2] which ends abruptly, and is the last of the Tinnevelly ghāṭs. But though the name Mahendragiri is now applied to two distinct hills in Ganjam and Tinnevelly respectively, there is no reason to think that any such distinction was intended by the poet of the Rāmāyaṇa. On the contrary, the position of Mahendra in relation to Malaya and Sahya, as described in the passage quoted from the Laṅkākāṇḍa, leaves little room for doubt that 'Mahendra' of the Rāmāyaṇa is the famous Kula-parvata of the same name mentioned in the Bhuvana-kosha in juxtaposition with Malaya and Sahya, and that it embraced the entire chain of hills extending from Ganjam to Tinnevelly.

Malaya is, next to the Himavat, perhaps the most famous mountain in Sanskrit literature. It gives its name to the cooling breeze of the south which finds frequent mention in Indian poetry.[3]

[1] Pargiter, *The Geography of Rāma's Exile*, JRAS, 1894, pp. 261-262.

[2] Gaz. of Tinnevelly Dist., Vol. I, by H. R. Pate, 1917, p. 4.

[3] In Dhoyi's Pavanadūta, the breeze of Malaya carries

Sanskrit writers refer to it also as Śrîkhaṇḍādri, Chandanādri or Chandanāchala.[1] The Tamil name is Podigei or Podigai, the original of the Bettigo of Ptolemy.[2]

Like Mahendra, Malaya figures also in inscriptions (*e.g.*, the Nāsik Praśasti of Gautamîputra Sātakarṇi) though not so prominently as in literature.

Malaya is the hill *par excellence* of the Pāṇḍyas,[3] as Mahendra is of the Kaliṅgas, and Sahya that of the Aparāntas. The name is

a love message from a Gandharva maiden of the Far South to King Lakshmaṇa-sena of Bengal. 'Malayaja-śîtalā' is an epithet which is applied to his motherland by a great Bengali writer of recent times.

Malaya is the mountain where, according to the Rāmopākhyāna (Mbh. iii. 281.44 f.) the monkey host, sent by Sugrîva in quest of Sîtā, saw the vulture Sampāti, and from it Hanumat made his famous descent on Laṅkā. It should, however, be noted that in the Rāmāyaṇa the Vindhya is mentioned in connection with Sampāti, and the Mahendra in connection with the exploit of Hanumat.

According to the Bhāgavata Purāṇa (x. 79) the hermitage of Agastya stood on the summit of Malaya.

1 See Dhoyi's Pavana-dūta.

2 McCrindle, *Ptolemy*, 1927, 78.

3 According to Dhoyi the Pāṇḍya-deśa lay at a distance of only 4 miles from Śrîkhaṇḍādri, *i.e.*, the Malaya Hills.

Śrîkhaṇḍādreḥ parisaram atikramya gavyūtimātram
gantavyaste kimapi jagati maṇḍanam Pāṇḍyadeśaḥ.

As already stated the Pāṇḍya king had the epithet Malaya-dhvaja.

connected with the Dravidian word 'Mala' or 'Malei' meaning 'hill.'[1] From it are derived the designations of the country of Mo-lo-kü-t'a referred to by Hiuen Tsang, and the language called Malayalam spoken by the people of 'Mālabār.' The names of the rivers issuing from this Kula-parvata, *viz.*, Kṛitamālā or Vaigai (on which stands Madurā or Dakshiṇa Mathurā[2]), and Tāmraparṇî (on which stood Korkai or Kolkoi, and Kāyal, three miles lower down the river), enabled scholars to identify it with the portion of the Western Ghāṭs (south of the Kāverî) from the Nilgiris to the neighbourhood of Cape Comorin,[3] with the exception of the most southerly spur of the Travancore Hills. The king of the Pāṇḍyas is referred to in literature as the lord of the Malaya (*cf.* Podiya-verpan of Tamil literature and Malaya-dhvaja of the Mahābhārata[4]) just as the king of Kaliṅga receives the epithet of Mahendranātha.

[1] Hultzsch in *Ind. Ant.*, 1889, 240 f. Also IA, vii. 277.

[2] Dakshiṇa Mathurā āilā Kāmakoshṭhi haite,
tāhā dekhā haila eka Brāhmaṇa sahite,
sei vipra Mahāprabhur kaila nimantraṇa
Rāmabhakta sei vipra virakta mahājana.
Kṛitamālāya snāna kari āilā tāṅr ghare.
Chaitanya-Charitāmṛita, Madhyalilā, Ch. ix, p. 141. (*Cf.* N. Dey.)

[3] Pargiter, Mārk. P. 285.

[4] Kālidāsa, too, testifies to the intimate connection between 'Malayādri' and the Pāṇḍyas (*cf.* Raghu., iv.

Sahya, like Mahendra and Malaya, finds mention in the Nāsik Praśasti of Gautamîputra Śātakarṇi. In the Alina copperplate inscription of Sîlāditya VII of Valabhi, it is probably associated with the Vindhya, the two being mentioned as the breasts of the earth.[1] Kālidāsa describes it as "nitambamiva medinyāḥ" (Raghu., iv. 52), and connects it with the Aparāntas, *i.e.*, the people of Western India, and particularly of the Koṅkaṇ.[2] The Purāṇas describe it as the source of the Godāvarî and its tributary, the Vañjulā or Mañjirā; the Kṛishṇaveṇā or Kṛishṇā and its tributaries the Bhîmarathî or Bhîmā and the Tuṅgabhadrā; and the Kāverî. It has, therefore, been correctly identified with the northern portion of the Western Ghāṭs from the Tāptî down to the Nilgiris. Ptolemy apparently divides it into two parts. To the northern part—the source of the river of Masulipatam (Maisolos), *i.e.*, the Godāvarî or the Kṛishṇā,—he gives the name of the Oroudian mountains.[3] The name is considered

46.49). In Raghu., iv. 51, Malaya is associated with Dardura—stanāviva diśastasyāḥ śailau Malaya-Dardurau.

[1] Fleet, *Corpus Inscriptionum Indicarum*, III, pp. 176, 184.

[2] 'Aparānta' has a wider and a narrower denotation. In its wider sense it means all India lying west of the Madhya-deśa; in the narrower sense only the Koṅkaṇ.

[3] Ptolemy, vii. 1.37, Majumdār's ed., pp. 81, 103.

to be equivalent to 'Vaidūrya' of Sanskrit literature, which the Mahābhārata associates with the rivers Payoshṇî and Narmadā.[1] The southern part of the Sahya is known to Ptolemy as the Adeisathron range, and is described by him as the source of the Khaberos (Kāverī).[2]

The **Śuktimat** is the least known among the mountain ranges of Ancient India.[3] According to the Mārkaṇḍeya Purāṇa it is the source of the Ṛishikulyā, the Kumārî, the Mandagā, the Mandavāhinî, the Kṛipā and the Palāśinî. Variant names of the rivers are given in some of the other Purāṇas including the Vāyu copy consulted by Alberuni.[4] The Vāmana Purāṇa omits these altogether, and mentions the Śunî and the Sudāmā among rivers issuing from the Śuktimat range. Further it confounds the rivers of Śukti with those rising in the Malaya.[5] In view of all

1 Mbh. iii. 121. 16-19:
sa Payoshṇyāṁ naraśreshṭhaḥ snātvā vai bhrātṛibhiḥ saha
Vaidūrya-parvatañchaiva Narmadāñcha mahānadîm
Vaidūrya-parvataṁ dṛishṭvā Narmadāṁ avatîrya cha

2 Ptolemy, vii, 1.35.

3 It is the only Kula-parvata which is not referred to in the Nāsik Praśasti of Gautamîputra Śātakarṇi. Kālidāsa, too, ignores it in the account of Raghu's conquests.

4 Kūrma, Pūrvabhāga, 46. 38-49; Matsya, 114. 32. Alberuni, i. 257 (Ch. XXV).

5 Vāmana, xiii. 32-33.

this confusion it is difficult to say which rivers actually issue from the Śuktimat. The uncertainty in regard to the names of most of the rivers renders their identification difficult, and makes the precise location of the parent range almost a hopeless task. Abul Fazl seems to regard the Śuktimat (as well as the other Kula-parvatas) as running from east to west, and makes it the dividing line between Kaser and Tāmravarṇa, two of the nine divisions of Bhārata.[1] But his account of the position of the *Nava-khaṇḍa* and the seven mountains is, in the main, not borne out by any early Indian author, and is indeed in conflict with what is known about them from other sources.

According to Cunningham [2] Śuktimat is the mountain range to the south of Sehoa and Kānker, which gives rise to the Mahānadî (=Śuktimatî according to him), the Pairi and the Seonath rivers, and forms the boundary between Chattisgarh and Bastar. Pargiter rejects this view as the great archaeologist's premises are unsafe and his conclusion confounds the Śuktimat with the Mahendra range. But it is by no means clear that the Mahendra range extended as far as the source of the Pairi and the Mahānadî. The really weak point in Cunningham's theory is the

[1] *Ain-i-Akbari*, III, pp. 30-31.

[2] Pargiter, Mārk. P., p. 285. *Arch. Survey Reports*, XVII, pp. 24, 26, and map at the end.

tacit assumption of a connection between Mount Śuktimat and the river Śuktimatî, and the identification of the latter with the Mahānadî. As a matter of fact the Śuktimatî takes its rise, not from the Śuktimat, but from the Vindhyan chain, using the word Vindhyan in its wider sense. Cunningham does not stand alone in his view that the Śukti Mountain is the source of the Śuktimatî. Beglar, too, makes the same mistake. Identifying the Śuktimatî with the Sakri, a tributary of the Ganges (east of Gayā), the Ṛishikulyā with the Kiyul, another tributary of the Ganges, east of the Sakri, and the Kumārî with the Kaorhari, he places Mount Śuktimat in the north of the Hazaribagh District.[1] The identifications are rejected by Pargiter [2] who points out that the Śuktimatî is not connected with Mt. Śuktimat, that Sakri is not the equivalent of Śuktimatî, but of Śakulî, and that the hills in the north of Hazaribagh are not remarkable, being rather the termination of the Vindhya range than a separate system. The last objection is not quite valid because the Śuktimat, too, is not a remarkable range and is rarely mentioned in literature. It is the only Kula-parvata which does not find mention in the Nāsik Praśasti of Gautamîputra Śātakarṇi. As to the objection that the Hazaribagh hills are not a separate system it may be

[1] *Arch. S. R.*, VIII, pp. 124, 125.

[2] Mārk. P. (trans.), 285.

pointed out that the *Kula-parvata* Pāriyātra, too, is not a separate system, but part of the Vindhyan chain.

Pargiter was at first inclined to identify Śuktimat with either the Aravalli Mt. or the southern part of the Eastern Ghāṭs. But he finally preferred the Garo, Khāsi and Tipperah hills in Eastern India,[1] "for Bhîma in his conquests in that quarter marched from Himavat towards Bhallāṭa and conquered the Śuktimat Mountain," and "the river Lohita and the country Kāmarupa, were known." Pargiter ignores the fact that Bhîma did not cross the Lohita or Lauhitya (Brahmaputra). The identification of the rivers Kumārî and Kṛipā issuing from Śuktimat (with Someśvarî and Kapilî) suggested by him, is also hardly satisfactory.

C. V. Vaidya identified the Śuktimat with the Kāthiāwāḍ range.[2] The Junāgaḍh inscription of Rudradāman no doubt mentions a Palāśinî as issuing from that range, and we know that Palāśinî is the name of one of the rivers rising in the Śukti Mountain. But the other rivers springing from the Śuktimat cannot be identified, and the evidence of the Mahābhārata points to some range between Indraprastha (Delhi) and Lauhitya (Brahmaputra) as the real Śuktimat.[3]

1 *Ibid*, p. 306.

2 *Epic India*, p. 276.

3 The mountain is mentioned in the account of the

Dr. R. C. Majumdār [1] and Mr. Hārit Krishna Dev [2] propose to identify the Śuktimat with the Sulaiman range. We are told that the two names closely resemble each other, that Kūpā, one of the streams issuing from the Suktimat, sounds very much like Kubhā (the Kābul river), and that Kumārî, Mandagā, Mandavāhinî, Palāśinî, Ṛishikulyā and Bhallāṭa with which Śukti is associated, are equivalent to Kunār, Helmand, Panjshir, Euaspla and Bhalanas respectively. It is further suggested that the epic list of places visited by Bhîma and his brothers was not drawn up strictly according to geographical position, and that, therefore, the evidence of the Mahābhārata cannot be a valid objection against the identity of Śukti with Sulaiman which is the only extensive range besides the Assam Hills, which has not been appropriated to the Kula-parvatas mentioned in the Bhuvana-kosha.

But the philological equations proposed above are, with one exception, hardly tenable.[3] As to the equation Kūpā = Kubhā, it is to be remembered

Dig-vijaya of Bhîma who started from the Pāṇḍu capital and marched eastwards as far as the Lauhitya.

> evaṁ bahuvidhān deśān vijigye Bharatarshabha
> Bhallāṭamabhito jigye Śuktimantañcha parvatam.
> (Mbh. ii. 30. 5.)

1 *Pro. Second Oriental Conference*, 1923, p. 609 f.

2 *Ibid*, p. ci; ZDMG, Leipzig, 1922, p. 281 n.

3 Jayaswal, *Pro. Second Oriental Conference*, 1923,

that the form Kūpā occurring in the extant Vāyu (and Brahmāṇḍa), is not met with in the Vāyu text consulted by Alberuni. That text and many extant Purāṇas have Kirpā,[1] Kṛipā[2] or Kshiprā[3] which obviously cannot be equated with Kubhā. Moreover, we have actually a Kopā,[4] a Kumārî[5] and a Parās[6] (Palāśinî ?) in Eastern India. Whatever we may think of the evidence of the Mahābhārata, the fact should not be ignored that Sulaiman, as pointed out by Pargiter and shown in the early part of this chapter, was considered to be a portion of the Himavat, the Varsha-parvata. The Kula-parvatas are expressly stated by Rājaśekhara to be

1 Alberuni, i. 257.

2 Matsya, 114. 32.

3 Kūrma, Pūrvabhāga, 46. 39.

4 Or Sāl, a tributary of the Dvārakā or Bāblā (O'Malley, Birbhum, 1910, p. 5).

5 The Kāsāi receives the waters of the Kumārî at Ambikānagar.

(O'Malley's Bankura, 1908, p. 7, *cf*. Coupland's Manbhum, 1911, p. 7.)

6 M. G. Hallett, Ranchi, 1917, p. 6. It is a tributary of the 'Koel.' The name Koel, we are told, is a common designation for river in Chota Nāgpur. It may refer to the Ṛishikulyā which is also a common river-name in the Purāṇas, being the designation of at least two streams —one rising in the Mahendra and the other in the Śuktimat. It is interesting to note that the Koel unites with the Sankh to form the Brāhmaṇî. In the Purāṇas Śaṅkha and Śukti are associated together (Mārk. 58. 24—Śaṅkha-Śuktyādi-Vaidūrya-śailaprānta-charāścha ye).

in the Kumārî Dvîpa whose furthest limit according to the Skanda Purāṇa was the Pāriyātra.[1] Further, if the Śuktimat be really the mountain range which runs south from the Hindukush, is not the omission of the Suvāstu, Gomatî and Krumu from the list of its rivers rather inexplicable?

The really important clues in regard to the identity of the Śuktimat are its association with Bhallāṭa and with 'Śaṅkha' and "Vaidūrya śaila" (Mārk. 58. 24). The Mahābhārata as well as the Jātakas seems to connect Bhallāṭa with Kāsi.[2] The Kalki Purāṇa, while describing the march of a victorious army, mentions Bhallāṭa-nagara just before Kāñchanî purî, the hill fortress of the Nāgas, which is doubtless identical with 'purîṁ Kāñchanikām' governed by Pravîra, the son of Vindyāśakti, in the third century A.D.[3] A tribe called Phyllitai is mentioned by Ptolemy as living in Central India.[4] These indications would point

[1] Skanda Purāṇa, Kumārikā-khaṇḍa, Ch. 39. 113: "Pāriyātrasya chaivārvākkhaṇḍaṁ Kaumārikaṁ smṛitam."

[2] Mbh. ii. 30. 5-7:

Bhallāṭamabhito jigye Śuktimantaṁ cha parvatam
Pāṇḍavaḥ sumahāvîryo balena balināṁ varaḥ
sa Kāsirājaṁ samare Subāhum anivartinam
vaśe chakre mahābāhur Bhîmo bhîma-parākramaḥ,

Jātaka No. 504 mentions a Bhallāṭiya as king of Benares.

[3] Kalkî Purāṇa, iii. 7. 36; iii. 14.3f.

Cf. Pargiter, *Dynasties of the Kali Age*, p. 50.

[4] Ptolemy, vii. 1.66. 'Phyllitai' sounds very much like Bhallāṭa.

to the central, and not the easternmost or north-western, part of India as the place where Bhallāṭa, and consequently Suktimat, were situated. And this accords with the Purāṇic evidence about the connection of Sukti with Saṅkha and Vaidūrya. The suggestion of N. Dās that the name Suktimat is preserved in the Suktel river which joins the Mahānadî, near Sonpur, and also in the Sakti Hills in Raigarh, C. P., seems plausible.[1] 'Sakti' actually stands midway between 'Sankh' and Vaidūrya which the Mahābhārata places in the neighbourhood of the Payoshṇî and the Narmadā. The name Suktimat was probably applied to the chain of hills that extends from Sakti in Raigarh, C. P., to the Dalma Hills in Manbhum drained by the Kumārî, and perhaps even to the hills in the Santhal Parganas washed by the affluents of the Bāblā.

Riksha and **Vindhya.**

The great chain of mountains along the Narmadā, which separates Northern India from the Deccan, is probably mentioned in the Kaushîtaki Upanishad under the name of Dakshiṇa Parvata.[2] At the present day the whole range is known by the name of the Vindhyas. In the

[1] *A Note on the Ancient Geography of Asia compiled from Vālmîki's Rāmāyaṇa* (1896), p. 51. See also Imp. Gaz., Atlas volume, plate 39.

[2] Kaush. Up., ii. 8.

period of the epics and the Purāṇas, however, different parts of the range had distinctive names, and ranked as separate Kula-parvatas. These names were Ṛiksha, Vindhya (proper) and Pāriyātra or Pāripātra, all of which find mention in the Nāsik Praśasti of Gautamîputra Sātakarṇi.[1] The first two are referred to by Ptolemy as the Ouxenton (Ṛikshavant) and the Ouïndion (Vindhya) ranges.

The Ṛiksha is probably so called because it stood in a territory which abounded in bears (*ṛikshas*).[2] There is a good deal of confusion in the *Bhuvana-kosha* section of the Purāṇas between the two Kula-parvatas—Ṛiksha and Vindhya. While the Vishṇu, Brahma, and some other texts describe the former as the source of the Tāpî, Payoshṇî and Nirvindhyā, and the latter as the source of the Narmadā, Daśārṇā, etc., the Kūrma, Matsya, Brahmāṇḍa, Vāmana and Vāyu texts, including that known to Alberuni, reverse the order, making the Ṛiksha the source of the Narmadā, Daśārṇā, etc., and the Vindhya the source of the Tāpī or Tāptî group. The *Bhuvana-kosha* underwent such textual corruption

[1] Rapson, *Andhra Coins*, p. xxxiii. The Prākṛita forms are Achavata, Vijha and Parivāta.

[2] Ṛikshadvîpa-samākulā.—Revākhaṇḍa, vi. 36.
asti Pauravadāyādo Vidurathasutaḥ prabho
Ṛikshaiḥ saṁvarddhito vipra Ṛikshavatyatha parvate.—Mbh., xii. 49. 76.

even in the time of Alberuni that little reliance can be placed on it in determining the identity of the two Kula-parvatas, Ṛiksha and Vindhya.

No conclusion regarding the relative position of Ṛiksha and Vindhya can also be drawn from the constant association of the former with the Narmadā[1] and that of the latter with the Revā,[2]

[1] Ṛikshavantaṁ giriśreshṭhamadhyāste Narmadāṁ pivan
(Rām., Laṅk., 27. 9.)

puraścha paśchāchcha yathā mahānadî
tam Ṛikshavantaṁ girimetya Narmadā.
(Mbh., xii. 52. 32.)

sa Narmadā-rodhasi śîkarārdrair marudbhirānartitanaktamāle
niveśayāmāsa vilaṅghitādhvā kāntaṁ rajo dhūsaraketu sainyam
athoparishṭād bhramarair bhramadbhiḥ prāksūchitāntaḥ-salila-praveśaḥ
nirdhauta-dānāmalagaṇḍabhittirvanyaḥ saritto gaja unmamajja
niḥśesha vikshālita dhātunāpi vaprakriyām Ṛikshavatastaṭeshu
nîlorddhvarekhā-śabalena śaṁsan dantadvayenāśmavikuṇṭhitena.
(Raghu, Ch. 5, 42-44.)

[2] Vindhyasyāvandhyakarmmā śikhara-taṭa-patat-pāṇḍu-Revāmbu-rāser......
(Fleet, *C.I.I.*, 154.)

śrūyatāṁ dvija-śārdūlāḥ kāraṇaṁ yena kandaram
Vindhyasyehāgato ramyaṁ Revāvāri-kaṇokshitam.
(Mārk. P., iv. 22.)

Revāṁ drakshyasyupalavishame Vindhyapāde viśîrṇām.
(Meghadūta, 19.)

for, though the Bhāgavata[1] and the Vāmana Purāṇas[2] seem to distinguish between the two rivers, the Revā-khaṇḍa regards them as one and the same,[3] a fact borne out also by incidental references in the Bhāgavata itself.[4]

More fruitful results may be obtained by an examination of the evidence of Ptolemy and the inscriptions, and certain *incidental* references in the Mahābhārata, the Purāṇas, the Harivaṁśa and the commentary of Nîlakaṇṭha. It will be seen that the name Ṛiksha is invariably applied to the *central* part of the chain lying *north* of the Narmadā, while the *eastern* part together with the hills standing *south* of the Narmadā and extending as far as the ocean, bore the name of Vindhya. Ptolemy, for instance, describes the Ouxenton (Ṛikshavant) as the source of the Toundis, the Dosaron and the Adamas.[5] The identification of these rivers with

1 Bhāgavata, 5. 19. 17.

2 Vāmana, xiii. 25-30.

3 kimarthaṁ Narmadā proktā
Reveti cha kathaṁ smṛitā.
(Revākhaṇḍa, 5. 7. *Cf. Ind. Ant.*, 1887, 253.)
Narakāntakarî Revā satîrthā viśvapāvanî
Narmadā dharmadā chāstu śarmadā Pārtha te sadā.
(*Ibid*, 229. 28.).

4. praviśya Revāmagamad yatra Māhishmatîpurî (Bhāg. x. 79). In the Harivaṁśa (Vishṇu Parva, 38. 14 f.) Narmadā is the name of the river which flows past Māhishmatî.

5 Ptolemy, VII, i, 39-41.

the Brāhmaṇî, the Vaitaraṇî and the Suvarṇarekhā, has little to support it. Dosaron sounds very much like the Daśārṇā (modern Dhasan near Saugor in C.P.) which actually occurs in the list of rivers issuing from the Ṛiksha as given in many Purāṇas, including the Vāyu copy used by Alberuni. The position assigned to the mouth of the river by Ptolemy is no insuperable objection against the proposed identity, because the western geographer had a very wrong idea about the configuration of India, and many of its mountains and rivers are 'hopelessly out of position.'[1] While the Ouxenton is connected with the Dosaron (Daśārṇā or Dhasan near Saugor), the Ouïndion (Vindhya) is represented as the source not only of the Namados (Narmadā) but also of the Nanagouna (Tāptî).[2] This proves that while the Ṛiksha lay in the region of the Central Vindhyas, near Saugor, the Vindhya proper, in the days of Ptolemy, comprised the chains at the source of the Narmadā and the Tāptî.

The connection of the Ṛiksha with the Central Vindhyas lying north of the Narmadā appears clear also from Indian evidence. Thus the Vāyu Purāṇa[3] represents a chief named Jyāmagha as

[1] *Cf.* Ptolemy, Majumdār's ed., p. 76.

[2] *Ibid*, VII. i. 31-32, pp. 102-103. *Cf.* Tāpi nāma nadî cheyaṁ Vindhyamūlād viniḥsṛitā (Prabhāsa Khaṇḍa, 11, 108).

[3] Vāyu, 95. 31.

crossing the Ṛiksha on his way from Narmadānūpa[1] to Śuktimatî, the capital of the Chedis, which lay to the north in the direction of the Yamunā. The Harivaṁśa refers to the city of Māhishmatî (Māndhāta ?), the capital of Narmadānūpa, as nestling under the shelter of Mount Ṛikshavat (Ṛikshavantam upāśritā). Nîlakaṇṭha, commenting on the Harivaṁśa, Vishṇuparva, Chap. 38, verse 7,

> Vindhy-arkshavantāvabhito
> dve puryau parvatāśraye
> niveśayatu yatnena
> Muchukunda suto mama,

says 'Vindhyasyottarataḥ Ṛikshavato dakshiṇata ityarthaḥ' implying that the two cities mentioned in the verse lay *north* of the Vindhyas and *south* of the Ṛiksha. The Bhāgavata places the hermitage of Atri, on the Ṛiksha,[2] and we learn from the Rāmāyaṇa that Atri's hermitage lay not far from

[1] The district on the Narmadā of which Māhishmatî was the capital (Raghu, vi. 37-43).

[2] Brahmaṇā choditaḥ sṛishṭāv-Atrir Brahmavidāṁ varaḥ
saha patnyā yayāv-Ṛikshaṁ Kulādriṁ tapasi sthitaḥ
tasmin prasūnastavaka-palāśāśoka-kānane
vārbhiḥ sravadbhirudghushṭe Nirvindhyāyāḥ samantataḥ.

(Bhāgavata, IV, i, 14-15.)

This Nirvindhyā need not be the river of the same name belonging to the Tāpî group. There was another Nirvindhyā which lay on the way from Vidiśā (Besnagar near Bhilsa) to Ujjayinî (Meghadūta, i. 25-29).

Chitrakūṭa.[1] The Nalopākhyāna of the Mahābhārata places the Ṛiksha mountain between Avantî and Dakshiṇāpatha.[2] On the other hand it expressly connects the Vindhya with the Payoshṇî [3]—a river of the Tāpî or Tāptî group. The association of the Vindhya with the region to the south of the Narmadā testified to by Nîlakaṇṭha and the author of the Nalopākhyāna of the Mahābhārata, is further confirmed by the popular belief that Sātpurā means seven sons or seven folds of the Vindhya.[4] In the famous Mandasor stone inscription of Yaśodharman and Vishṇu-vardhana we have reference to a tract of land, "containing many countries, which lies between the Vindhya (mountains), from the slopes of the summits of which there flows the pale mass of the waters of (the river) Revā, and the mountain Pāriyātra, on which the trees are bent down in (their) frolicsome leaps by the long-tailed monkeys (and

[1] Rāmāyaṇa, ii. 117. 5.

[2] ete gachchhanti bahavaḥ panthāno Dakshiṇāpatham
Avantîm Ṛikshavantañcha samatikramya parvatam.
(Mbh., iii. 61. 21.)

[3] esha Vindhyo mahāśailaḥ Payoshṇî cha samudragā.
(Mbh., iii. 61. 22.)

Cf. Prabhāsa-Khaṇḍa, 11-108, cited above.

[4] C. P. Dist. Gaz., Betul, by Russell, 1907, p. 258. *Cf.* the name Indhyādri, given to the hills at Ajaṇṭā (Bomb. Gaz., I. ii. 354), and "Bandah," *i.e.*, Vindhya (Gāwilgarh hills) in the *Ain-i-Akbari*, ii. 228.

stretches) up to the ocean" (Sindhu).[1] If the Vindhya (when distinguished from the Pāriyātra) means the range east of Bhopal, as suggested by Pargiter, then the countries between it and the Pāriyātra must be inland territory which cannot be said to extend to the ocean, or even to the rivers called *Sindhu*. But if Vindhya includes the hills to the south of the Narmadā, then the region between it and the Pāriyātra does extend to the ocean. It would, however, be a mistake to think that the Vindhya lay *wholly* to the south of the Narmadā, because an inscription of Ananta-varman Maukhari mentions that mountain as extending up to and including the Nāgārjunî Hill in the Gayā District.[2]

The question of the inclusion of the Amarakaṇṭaka mountain—the source of the Narmadā—presents a real difficulty. We have seen that Ptolemy makes it a part of the Ouïndion (Vindhya) range. But the Revā-khaṇḍa of the Skanda Purāṇa, with equal clearness, makes it a part of the Ṛiksha.[3] The truth seems to be that ancient

[1] Fleet, *C.I.I.*, 154.

[2] *Ibid*, pp. 227, 228.

[3] tataḥ sā Ṛikshaśailendrāt phenapuñjāṭṭahāsinî
viveśa Narmadā devī samudraṁ saritāmpatim
—Revākhaṇḍa, v. 51.

Soṇo Mahānadaśchaiva Narmadā Surasā Kritā
Mandākinî Daśārṇā cha Chitrakūṭā tathaiva cha
Ṛikshapāda-prasūtāstāḥ sarvā vai Rudra-sambhavāḥ
—*ibid*, iv. 46-48.

Hindu writers commonly regarded Vindhya and Ṛiksha as interchangeable terms. But one fact is clear. While the name Vindhya was loosely applied to the whole chain of hills from Gujarāṭ to the Gayā District, lying on *both* sides of the Narmadā,[1] the Ṛiksha, when referred to incidentally in literature, is invariably associated with the Middle Narmadā region of which Māhishmatî was the most important city, and the Daśārṇā (Dhasan) a notable river. The Vindhya, when distinguished from the Ṛiksha, denotes the chain lying south of the Narmadā, as Nîlakaṇṭha suggests.

Pāriyātra. We now come to the Pāriyātra ("the mountains which curve around") or Pāripātra (" the mountains shaped like an enclosing receptacle ") which marks, according to the Skanda Purāṇa, the furthest limit of Kumārî Khaṇḍa—the heart and centre of Bhārata-varsha. The earliest

[1] See particularly Ptolemy's association of the Ouïndion with both the Namados and the Nanagouna, and the Harivaṁśa verse ii. 38.20, ' ubhayor Vindhyayoḥ pāde nagayo stāṁ mahāpurîm,' where we have reference to *two* Vindhyas, *viz.*, the Vindhya proper and the Ṛiksha. Note also the name 'Nir Vindhyā,' *i.e.*, issuing out of the Vindhya, applied to rivers on both sides of the Narmadā. One of the Nirvindhyās is associated with Ujjayinî and Avantî and hence lay north of the Narmadā. Another belongs to the Tāpî-Payoshṇî group. *Cf.* also the Vindhya-dakshiṇa-pāda of the Kāvya-Mîmāṁsā, p. 94; and Rāmāyana, iv. 52.

reference to the mountain is probably that contained in the Dharma-Sūtra of Bodhāyana, where it forms the boundary line between Āryāvarta and the land of the barbarians.[1] Even in the days of the Mahābhārata it was the favourite resort of one of the most important of the 'barbarian' tribes, *viz.*, the Nishādas.[2] The earliest epigraphic reference to it is probably that occurring in the Nāsik Praśasti of Gautamîputra Śātakarṇi. It also finds prominent mention in the Mandasor inscription of Yaśodharman and Vishṇuvardhana. The mountain apparently gave its name to the famous Po-li-ye-ta-lo or Pāriyātra[3] country ruled by a Vaiśya king in the days of Hiuen Tsang. The names of the rivers issuing from it, *viz.*, the Mahî Varṇāśā or Parṇāśā,[4] Charmanvatî, Siprā, Sindhu[5] and Vetravatî, clearly support the view of Pargiter that it corresponds to the portion of

[1] I. i. 25: "Prāgadarśanāt pratyak Kālakavanād dakshiṇena Himavantam udak Pāriyātram etad Āryāvartam."

[2] Mbh., xii. 135.3.5.

[3] *Cf.* Harsha-charita (Cowell and Thomas, trans., pp. 210-211), and Bṛihat Saṁhitā, xiv. 4.

[4] The modern Banās, a tributary of the Chambal or Charmanvatî (Pargiter). The reading "Venvā" (instead of Varṇāśā or Parṇāśā) is apparently incorrect.

[5] Either Kali Sindhu, a tributary of the Chambal, or Sindh, a tributary of the Jumna, lying between the Chambal and Betwa (Vetravatî).

the modern Vindhya range west of Bhopal, together with the Aravalli mountains.

Besides the *Kula-parvatas*, the Purāṇas mention a number of smaller hills (**Kshudra-parvata**) which are situated near the former (bhūdharā ye samîpagāḥ). They may be conveniently grouped under the following heads :—

(1) Hills associated with the Eastern Ghāṭs—*e.g.*, (*a*) Śrî-parvata. In the *Agni Purāṇa* Śrî-parvata is mentioned next after " Kāverī-saṅgamaḥ " (Kāverī-saṅgamaṁ puṇyaṁ Śrī-parvatamataḥ śriṇu, cxiii, 3-4). " It overhangs the Krishṇā in the Karnool District " and is usually identified by scholars with Siriṭana of the Nāsik Praśasti. It was famous as the site of the Śaiva shrine of Mallikārjuna.

(*b*) Pushpagiri.—It lay eight miles to the north of Cuddapah.[1]

(*c*) Veṅkaṭa.—It is in Draviḍa forming the boundary line between the Tamil and Telugu countries.[2]

(*d*) Aruṇāchala [3] or Śoṇāchala.—It stands on the river Kampā which flows past Kāñchî.

[1] *Ep. Ind.*, iii. 24. Pargiter was unable to identify it.

[2] Smith, EHI[4], p. 456: ' Draviḍeshu mahāpuṇyaṁ drishṭvādriṁ Veṅkaṭam Prabhuḥ.' (Bhāgavata, x. 79.)

[3] See *Aruṇāchala Māhātmya* of the Skanda-purāṇa, Ch. iii, 59-61; iv. 9, 13, 21, 37.

(*e*) Ṛishabha.—It is placed by the Bhāgavata Purāṇa (x. 79) between the Kāverî and Madurā. The Mahābhārata (iii. 85. 21) places it in the Pāṇḍya country.

(2) Hills associated with Malaya.—The most important among them is the Dardura. Pargiter suggests its identification with the Nilgiris or the Palni Hills. The Raghuvaṁśa (iv. 51) refers to Malaya and Dardura as the breasts of the southern region. In the Sabhāparva of the Mahābhārata the Chola and Pāṇḍya kings offer sandal from Dardura.[1] A monkey chief according to Pargiter inhabited Dardura and drank of the river Parṇāśā. But the text calls the chief Dardura-saṅkāśo [2] which does not necessarily indicate that he resided in Dardura.

(3) Hills associated with Sahya,—*e.g.* (*a*) Vaidūrya [3] connected by the Mahābhārata with the Payoshṇî and the Narmadā, and identified by scholars with the Oroudian mountain mentioned by Ptolemy.

1 Mbh., ii. 52.34. Dardura is also mentioned in xiii. 165. 32. See also Pargiter, JRAS, 1894, 262.

2 Rām., Lanka, 26.42.

3 'Vaidūrya' apparently included the northernmost part of the Western Ghāṭs as the evidence of Ptolemy suggests. But it also included a part at least of the Sātpurā range as the Mahābhārata clearly indicates. It is the connecting link between the Sahya and the southern Vindhya with both of which it seems to have been confounded.

(*b*) Govardhana—the hill of Nāsik.[1]

(*c*) Devagiri—the "towering hill" of modern Daulatābād. Bomb. Gaz., I. ii. 501, 534.

(*d*) Krishṇagiri (Kaṇhagiri of the Nāsik inscription)—modern Kanheri.[2]

(*e*) Trikuṭa.—It is placed in the Aparānta country. It gave its name to the Traikuṭaka dynasty.[3]

(*f*) Kolva, probably the hill near Kolhapur.[4]

(*g*) Ṛishyamūka.—It stretched, according to Pargiter, from Ahmadnagar to beyond Naldrug and Kalyāni, dividing the Mañjirā and the Bhîmā. Fleet (IA, 6,85) refers to it as a hill on the north of Hampe.

(*h*) Mālyavat.—It lay in the Kishkindhyā country, and is identified by Pargiter with the curved lines of hills near Kupal, Mudgal, and Raichur.

1 *Cf.* Rapson, *Andhra Coins*, pp. xxix, xlvii, lvi. For another Govardhana, see Rice, *Mysore and Coorg*, 138-41.

2 *Ibid*, xxxiii. It is in Sālsette, Bomb. Gaz., I. ii.9. The mountain is also mentioned in the Rāmāyaṇa (vi. 26.30).

3 See Raghu. iv. 59, and Rapson, *Andhra Coins*, lxiii. There is another Trikuṭa in Kashmir (Prinsep, *Origin of the Sikh Power*, Ch. 3).

4 See Bhāg. P., v. 19.16. Kollagiri is placed in southern India in the description of Arjuna's march with the sacrificial horse (in the Aśvamedha-parva). *Cf.* Kollagiri in Bomb. Gaz., I. ii. 497; Mbh., ii. 31. 68.

(*i*) Prasravaṇa.—It is associated with the Godāvarî and the Mandākinî (Araṇya, 64. 10-14) as well as with a Vindhya in the extreme south of India (Rām. Kishk., 52.31), and seems to have also included the Mālyavat.[1] It was perhaps the general name of the mountain chains stretching from the Mandākinî and the Godāvarî to the southern sea.

(*j*) Gomanta.—It lay in a *Vivara* of the Sahya. To its north stood Vanavāsi.[2] It is, therefore, to be placed in the Mysore region, and not near Nāsik as suggested by Pargiter.

(4) Hills associated with the western Vindhyas.

(*a*) Urjjayanta.—It is the Girnār Mountain situated on the east side of Junāgaḍh in Kāṭhiāwāḍ (Surāshṭra)[3] which figures so prominently in the Junāgaḍh Rock inscriptions of Rudradāman and Skanda Gupta. The mountain is also mentioned in the Mahābhārata (iii. 88.23) and is probably hinted at in the Ṛig Veda (ii. 13.8).

(*b*) Raivataka.—It is the hill opposite to Ūrjayat or Girnār.[4] In literature it is associated with the Yādava tribe.

[1] See JRAS, 1894, *Geography of Rāma's Exile*, pp. 256-258.

[2] Harivaṁśa, Vishṇu-parva, 39. 62-64.

[3] Fleet, *CII*, p. 57.

[4] Fleet, *CII*, 64 n. Paśchimabhāge, Skanda Purāṇa, Vastr. 1.68.

(*c*) Arbuda.—Mount Abu at the south end of the Aravalli Range. We have a detailed account of the mountain in the Arbuda Khanda of the Skanda Purāṇa.

(*d*) Govardhana—the famous hill near the Jumna.

(5) Hills associated with the central Vindhyas, *e.g.* (*a*) Amarakaṇṭaka. It forms the eastern peak of Mekala or the Maikala Range which is "the connecting link between the great hill systems of the Vindhyas and Sātpurās," and stretches from the Khairāgarh State in C.P. to the Rewah State. It is the source of the Narmadā, the Soṇa and the Mahānadî.

(*b*) Kolāhala.—It is placed by Pargiter between Panna and Bijawar in Bundelkhand. The Mahābhārata connects it with the river Śuktimatî (Ken).

(*c*) Chitrakūṭa.—It is the name of a famous hill lying 65 miles W. S. W. of Allahabad (JRAS, 1894, 239). The Mahābhārata associates it with Kālañjara (Mbh., iii. 85.56).

(6) Hills associated with the eastern Vindhyas, *e.g.*, Pravaragiri-Gorathagiri. It is the Barābar Hill (Fleet, *CII*, 222-223). The identification of Gorathagiri with the Barābar Hill was suggested by Jackson in JBORS, i. 159f. In the Maurya period it was known as Khalatika pavata. The name Gorathagiri is found in the Great Epic and

the inscription of Kharavela. The name Pravaragiri occurs in a Maukhari inscription.

Pāṇḍava.—It is the name of one of the five hills of Rājagṛiha, mentioned prominently in Buddhist literature (Cunn., *AGI*, 530).

Vaibhrāja or Vaihāra.—It is also one of the five hills of Rājagṛiha mentioned in the epic and in Buddhist literature, modern Baibhāra.[1]

Vātasvana.—Bathan in South Bihār according to Beglar, *ASR* viii,. 46.

Mandāra—in the Bhāgalpur District (Fleet, *CII*, p. 211) situated about 35 miles south of Bhāgalpur (*ASR*, viii, 130).

(7) Hills in the Far East—

Kāmagiri.—Kāmākhyā in Assam.

Udayagiri.—It refers either to the real Udayagiri in Orissa or S. Bihār, or the mythical mountain, associated with Astagiri.

[1] The names of the five hills of Rājagṛiha mentioned in the Pāli annals of Ceylon are (in Sanskrit) Gṛidhrakūṭa, Ṛishigiri, Vaibhāra, Vipula and Pāṇḍava (Cunn., *AGI.*, 530). Of these only the second, third and probably also the fourth find mention in the Mahābhārata (ii. 21. 2). Gṛidhrakūṭa, identified by Marshall with Chhathāgiri (*ASI*, 1905-6, pp. 86-90) is probably "Chaityaka" of the Mahābhārata. Pāṇḍava, identified by Cunningham with Ratnagiri, is in that case Vṛishabha of the epic and Vṛishabha-dhvaja of the Purāṇas. The Mbh., ii. 22.45, however, connects the Pāṇḍavas with Chaityaka.

(8) Hills associated with the Himavat: Maināka, Krauñcha,[1] Hemagiri,[2] and Indraparvata (Mbh., ii. 30. 15).

(9) Hills whose identity is unknown: Vaidyuta, Svarasa, Tuṅgaprastha, Rochana, Kūṭaśaila, Kṛistasmara, Kora, Añjana, Jambu, Mānava, Sūrpa-karṇa, Vyāghra-mukha, Kharmaka, Karvaṭāśana, Sūryādri, Kumudādri, Maṇimegha, Kshurādri, Khañjana, Dhanushmat, Vashumat (Mārkaṇḍeya Purāṇa); Maṅgala-prastha, Vāridhāra, Droṇa, Gokāmukha (Bhāgavata Purāṇa).

[1] Pargiter, Mārk. P., 376 n. Krauñcha "appears to have been a portion of the Maināka mountains in the great Himavat mountain system." It is "the portion of the Himālaya chain bounding Nepāl at the extreme north-west."

[2] Pargiter, Mārk. P., 369 n.

PART III

HISTORY AND CHRONOLOGY

PART III

History and Chronology

CHAPTER VIII

Buddhism in Western Asia

Thanks to the active propaganda of Aśoka, and the pious zeal of missionaries and monks like Mahendra, Kāśyapa-Mātaṅga, Bodhi-dharma, Kumāra-jīva, Śānta-rakshita, Padma-sambhava, Atīśa and others of lesser note, Buddhism spread throughout Southern, Central, and Eastern Asia and the neighbouring Islands, where millions of people to this day revere the Śākya sage as their teacher and master. But Western Asia remains outside the spiritual empire of the Blessed One. The tide of Indian spiritual influence, it has been said, flowed eastwards rather than westwards. Nevertheless it is a fact that the vast region beyond the western frontiers of India came within the geographical horizon of Buddhist writers as early as the *Bāveru Jātaka* and possibly the *Sussondi Jātaka*, and its princes figure not inconspicuously in Buddhist inscriptions of the third century B.C. The records of Aśoka show that the eyes of the imperial missionary of Magadha were turned more to the West than to the East; and even the traditional account of early Buddhist proselytising efforts given in the chronicles of Ceylon,[1] does not omit to mention the country of the Yonas where Mahārakkhita "delivered in the midst of the people the '*Kālakārāma suttanta*,' in consequence of which a hundred and seventy thousand living beings attained to the reward of the path (of salvation) and ten thousand received the *pabbajjā*." It will perhaps be argued that the Yona country mentioned in the chronicles is to be identified with some district in the Kābul valley, and is not to be taken to refer to the realm of "Antiochos, the Yona king, and the kings, the neighbours of that Antiochos, namely, Ptolemy, Antigonos, Magas and Alexander," mentioned in the second and the thirteenth Rock Edicts of Aśoka. Rhys Davids, in fact, is inclined to regard the declaration in these edicts about the success of Aśoka's missionary propaganda in the realms of Yona princes as mere "royal rhodomontade." "It is quite likely," says he, "that the Greek kings are only thrown in by way of makeweight, as it were; and that no emissaries had been actually sent there at all."[2]

Alberuni,[3] however, writing in the eleventh century A.D. says, "In former times Khurāsān, Persis, Irāk, Mosul, the country up to the frontier of Syria, was Buddhistic, but then Zarathustra went forth from Ādharbaijān and preached Magism

[1] *Mahāvaṁsa*, Ch. xii.

[2] *Buddhist India*, p. 298.

[3] Sachau, *Alberuni's India*, Vol. I, p. 21.

in Balkh (Baktra). His doctrine came into favour with king Gushtasp, and his son Isfendiyād spread the new faith both in East and West, both by force and by treaties. He founded fire-temples through his whole Empire, from the frontiers of China to those of the Greek Empire. The succeeding kings made their religion (*i.e.* Zoroastrianism) the obligatory state-religion for Persis and Irāk. In consequence, the Buddhists were banished from those countries, and had to emigrate to the countries east of Balkh......Then came Islam." The above account may not be correct in all its particulars. The statement that Buddhism flourished in the countries of Western Asia before Zoroaster is clearly wrong. But the prevalence of the religion of Sākyamuni in parts of Western Asia in a period considerably anterior to Alberuni, and its supersession by Zoroastrianism and Islam may well be based upon fact. The antagonism of Buddhism to the fire-cult is hinted at in the *Bhūridatta Jātaka* (No. 543, Verses 138 f.).[1] It has even been suggested that Zoroastrian scriptures allude to disputes with the Buddhists.[2]

[1] *Cf.* Sikhiṁ hi devesu vadanti h'eke
āpaṁ milakkhā pana devam āhu
sabbe va ete vitathaṁ bhaṇanti
aggî na devaññataro na cāpo.
—Fausboll, *The Jātaka*, vi, 207.

[2] Sir Charles Eliot, *Hinduism and Buddhism*, iii,

Four centuries before Alberuni, Hiuen Tsang bore witness to the fact that Lang-kie (ka)-lo, a country subject to Persia, contained above 100 monasteries and more than 6,000 Brethren who applied themselves to the study of the Great and Little "Vehicles." Persia (Po-la-sse) itself contained two or three Saṅghārāmas, with several hundred priests, who principally studied the teaching of the Little Vehicle according to the Sarvāstivādin school. The *pātra* of Śākya Buddha was in this (country), in the King's palace.[1]

The Chinese pilgrim did not probably personally visit Persia. But no doubt need be entertained regarding the existence of Buddhist communities and Saṅghārāmas in Irān. Stein discovered a Buddhist monastery in "the terminal marshes of the Helmund" in Seistān.[2] Mānī, the founder of the Manichæan religion, who was born in A.D. 215-16, at Ctesiphon in Babylonia, and began to preach his gospel probably in A.D. 242, shows unmistakable traces of Buddhist influence.[3] In his book *Shābūrqān* (*Shapurakhan*) he speaks of the Buddha as a messenger of God. Legge and Eliot refer to a Manichæan treatise which has the

[1] Beal, *Records of the Western World*, Vol. II, pp. 277-278 ; Watters, *Yuan Chwang*, ii, 257.

[2] Sir Charles Eliot, *Hinduism and Buddhism*, iii, 3.

[3] *Ibid*, p. 446 ; *The Dacca University Journal*, Feb., 1926, pp. 108, 111; *JRAS.*, 1913, 69, 76, 81 ; E. J. Thomas, *The Life of Buddha*, xiii.

form of a Buddhist Sūtra. It speaks of Mānī as the Tathāgata and mentions Buddhas and the Bodhisattva. In his *History of Fine Art in India and Ceylon* [1] Dr. Vincent Smith refers to a picture of a four-armed Buddhist saint or Bodhisattva in the guise of a Persian with black beard and whiskers, holding a thunderbolt (vajra) in his left hand, which had been found at a place called Dandān-Uiliq in Turkestan. Such figures are undoubtedly the products of a type of Buddhism which must have developed in Irān, and enjoyed considerable popularity as late as the eighth century A.D. which is the date assigned by Dr. Smith to the fresco or distemper paintings on wood and plaster discovered at Dandān-Uiliq.

It is difficult to say to what extent Buddhist literature made its influence felt in Western Asia. Sir Charles Eliot points out the close resemblance between certain Manichæan works and the Buddhist *Suttas* and the *Pātimokkha*, and says that according to Cyril of Jerusalem, the Manichæan scriptures were written by one Scythianus and revised by his disciple Terebinthus who changed his name to Boddas.[2] He finds in this "jumble"

[1] P. 310.

[2] *Cf.* McCrindle, *Ancient India as described in Classical Literature*, p. 185.

"Terebinthus proclaimed himself learned in all the wisdom of the Egyptians and gave out that his name was no longer Terebinthus but that he was a new Buddha

allusions to Buddha, Sākyamuni and the Bo-tree. It may further be pointed out that some *Jātaka* tales show a surprising similarity to some of the stories in the *Arabian Nights*. The *Samugga Jātaka* (No. 436), for instance, tells the story of the demon (*dānava*) who put his beautiful wife in a box and so guarded her in order that she might not go astray. But this did not prevent her from taking pleasure with others. The tale in all its essentials recurs in the *Arabian Nights*.[1]

The *Jātaka* verse,

> "He his true bliss in solitude will find,
> Afar from woman and her treachery"

is comparable to the statement of the poet in the *Arabian Nights*:

> "Never trust in women ; nor rely upon their vows ;
> For their pleasure and displeasure depend upon their passions.
> They offer a false affection ; for perfidy lurks within their clothing."

(Buddas) and that he was born of a virgin. Terebinthus was the disciple of Scythianus, who was a Saracen born in Palestine and who traded with India."

[1] On reading the *JRAS.*, 1890, 504, I find that the suggestion is already made there. See also Olcott, *Stories from the Arabian Nights*, p. 3; Lane's *Arabian Nights*,

Whatever may be the case at the present day, in times gone by, Western Asia was clearly not altogether outside the sphere of the intellectual and spiritual conquests of Buddhism.

pp. 8-9. A similar story is found in Lambaka x, taraṅga 8 of the Kathā-sarit-sāgara ; Penzer, *The Ocean of Story*, Vol. V, pp. 151-152. " So attachment to women, the result of infatuation, produces misery to all men. But indifference to them produces in the discerning emancipation from the bonds of existence."

CHAPTER IX

A Note on the Vastrāpatha-Māhātmya of the Skanda Purāṇa

The value of the Purāṇas as "the most systematic record of Indian historical tradition" has long been recognised by scholars, and the dynastic lists contained in them have been largely utilised in reconstructing the political history of Ancient India. Unfortunately attention has hitherto been focussed mainly on the *Bhavishyānukīrtana* sections, and one famous author makes himself responsible for the dictum that "all the historical statements of the Purāṇas are given in the form of prophecy, in order to maintain the appearance of great antiquity in the books, which in their oldest forms were undoubtedly very ancient."[1] As the account of the "future" kings in these prophetic passages "stops with the imperial Guptas and their contemporaries," the value of the Purāṇic texts as sources of post-Gupta traditional history has not been sufficiently examined.

It will be our endeavour in this short note to call attention to a legend in the extant Skanda Purāṇa (Vaṅgavāsī Edition) in which we come

[1] Smith, EHI[4], p. 23.

across certain historical allusions that are not given in the form of prophecy, and can be made to yield information about kings who flourished long after the passing away of the Imperial Guptas.

In the Prabhāsa-khaṇḍa of the Skanda Purāṇa, there is a section called Vastrāpatha-māhātmya which is a collection of tales about the sacred sites of Vastrāpatha or Girnār in Surāshṭra or Kāthiāwāḍ. The most conspicuous features of this region are the Mount Raivataka and the river Suvarṇa-rekhā, or Svarṇa-rekhā [1] perhaps identical with the Suvarṇa-sikatā which is mentioned along with the Palāśinî in the Junāgaḍh Rock Inscription of the great Śaka Satrap Rudradāman.[2] Regarding the sanctity of this holy spot we have the following story :—

In the days of yore there lived in Kānyakubja (Kanauj) a king named B hoja.[3] Once upon a time there came to him a *Vanapāla* (Warden of the Forests) who said, " Sire (*deva*) I have seen a woman with the face of a doe roaming with a herd of deer in the forests at Raivataka." [4] The

[1] Etad Raivatakaṁ kshetraṁ Vastrāpatham iti smṛtam
Suvarṇarekhā yatrasthā nadî pātakanāśinî
(Prabhāsa-khaṇḍa, Vastrāpatha-kshetra-māhātmya, i. 2-3).

[2] *Ep. Ind.*, viii. 46.

[3] Kānyakubje mahākshetre rājā Bhojeti viśrutaḥ
Purā puṇyayuge dharmyaḥ prajā dharmeṇa śāsati
(Vastrāpatha-māhātmya, VI. 20).

[4] *Ibid*, verses 22 f., 127-129 : "Surāshṭradeśe bhavitā... mṛigī Raivatake girau."

king's curiosity was roused. Collecting his troops he marched towards Raivataka and encircled the hill with a net. The deer-maiden was captured by the *Balādhyaksha* (general), and was taken by the king to Kānyakubja, where she recounted the story of her previous births, and spoke about the spiritual efficacy of the holy waters of the Suvarṇarekhā. The king was much impressed with what he heard about Surāshṭra and its holy spots from the maiden and a Brāhmaṇa from Kurukshetra, and expressed his resolve to abdicate in favour of his son,[1] so that he might be free to undertake a pilgrimage to those sacred spots.

There are details in this, as in other priestly legends, which belong to the domain of fairy tales, and are absolutely unworthy of serious consideration. But there are three points which deserve examination. These are (1) the mention of a king Bhoja who reigned at Kanauj, (2) the connection of that king with Surāshṭra as evidenced by the appointment of a *Vanapāla*[2] and the despatch of an army,[3] and (3) his abdication in favour of his son.

As to the first, inscriptions discovered at Barah[4] (near Cawnpore), Daulatpurā[5] (in Jodhpur State), Deogaḍh[6] (in Jhansi), Gwalior,[7] Pehevā[8] (in

[1] *Ibid*, x. 15. [2] *Ibid*, vi. 22 f.

[3] *Ibid*, vi. 25 f. [4] *Ep. Ind.*, xix (1927), 15 f.

[5] *Ep. Ind.*, v, pp. 208 f. JRAS, 1909, p. 265.

[6] *Ep. Ind.*, iv. 309 f.

[7] *Ep. Ind.*, i. 157 f. ; xviii. 99. [8] *Ep. Ind.*, i. 184 f.

Karnal) and Āhār [1] (in Bulandshahr District), prove that there was actually in the Gurjara Pratihāra dynasty of Northern India a king named Bhoja who had his capital at Mahodaya or Kanauj [2] and whose dates probably ranged from V. S. 893 to H. S. 298, *i.e.*, A.D. 836 to 904-5. The name Bhoja was also borne by one of his grandsons, as we learn from the Bengal Asiatic Society's plate of the Mahārāja Vināyaka-pāla deva issued [3] from Mahodaya.

Regarding the second point we should note that Nāgabhaṭa II, grandfather of Bhoja, is known to have held the hill-forts of Ānarta (in Kāthiāwāḍ), [4] and the supremacy of Mahendrapāla I, son and successor of Bhoja, was acknowledged by Śrî Dhīika, Balavarman and his son Avanivarman

[1] Journal of the U. P. Historical Society, Vol. III. *The Ahar Stone Inscription* by C. D. Chatterjee.

[2] In *Ep. Ind.*, xix (p. 17), Mr. H. Śāstrī opines that Mahodaya was not Kānyakubja, and that Skandhāvāra does not mean 'rājadhānî.'

Regarding the identity of Mahodaya, see *Śabda-kalpa-druma*: "Mahodayaṁ puraviśeshaḥ—tatparyāyaḥ Kānyakubjaṁ Gādhipuraṁ Kauśaṁ Kuśasthalam iti Hemachandraḥ." *Cf.* Śrî Kānyakubja of the Khālimpur Ins. of Dharmapāla and Mahodaya-śrî of the Bhāgalpur plate of Nārāyaṇa pāla; also Bālarāmāyaṇa, Act X, 86-90, and Kāvya Mīmāṁsā, p. xxiii. As to Skandhāvāra, see Pavanadūta "Skandhāvāraṁ Vijayapuram ity unnatāṁ rājadhānîm.

[3] Kielhorn, Northern Ins., No. 544.

[4] Sāgar Tāl Ins., Arch. S.I.R., 1903-4, 281; *Ep. Ind.*, xviii, ed. by R. C. Majumdār, p. 108.

II Yoga who ruled over parts of the "Saurāshṭra Maṇḍala."[1] As (Vāhuka)dhavala, great-grandfather of Avanivarman II, claims to have defeated Dharma(pāla), the great rival of Nāgabhaṭa II, great-grandfather of Mahendra, it is not improbable that the family of Avanivarman II had entered into feudatory relations with the Imperial Pratihāras as early as the time of Nāgabhaṭa II, and it was apparently under his banner that Vāhukadhavala marched against Dharmapāla.[2] In view of the political relation between Surāshṭra and Kanauj existing from the time of Nāgabhaṭa II to that of his great-grandson Mahendrapāla, the episode of the Vastrāpatha-māhātmya acquires a new significance. The Haḍḍālā plates of the Chāpa Mahāsāmantādhipati Dharaṇīvarāha, a feudatory of the Rājādhirāja Mahîpāladeva,[3] supply us with an additional link in the chain connecting Kāthiāwāḍ with the Pratihāras of Kanauj.

Regarding point (3), *viz.*, that relating to the alleged abdication of Bhoja, king of Kanauj, we should refer to the anomaly presented by the inscription of the time of Mahendrapāla I, dated 893-94, and the Āhār stone inscription furnishing the dates 864-865,.865-866, 867-868, 886, 886-887, 888-889, 902-903 and 904-905 and purporting to belong to the reign of his father Bhoja. Mr. C. D.

[1] *Ep. Ind.*, ix. 1f.

[2] R. D. Banerji, *Bāṅgālāra Itihāsa*, p. 167.

[3] Kielhorn, *Northern Ins.*, No. 353.

Chatterjee seeks to explain the anomaly in two ways. " One of them is to assume that a portion of the (Āhār) inscription was engraved in A.D. 865-866 during the administration of Bhoja I, but other portions were added later on." The other is to surmise that " the mention of the different dates for the different gifts, brought together for record in one and the same inscription, indicates that there was a transfer to stone of a copy of all the deeds made on less durable materials, later than 904-905 A.D." But the possibility that Bhoja actually abdicated temporarily about A.D. 893 cannot be entirely excluded in view of the king's resolve alluded to in the Skanda Purāṇa :—

Tyaktvā rājyaṁ priyān putrān
pattyaśva-ratha-kuñjarān
putraṁ rājye pratishṭhāpya
gantavyaṁ niśchitaṁ mayā.[1]

In the Rājataraṅgiṇî we have the instance of king Ananta abdicating in favour of his son Kalasa and again resuming control over a part of the kingdom [2] There are certain indications which point to the fact that Bhoja I was not the only king of the Pratihāra line of Kanauj whose reign ran into that of his son. The reign of Vināyakapāla,

[1] Vastrāpatha-māhātmya, x. 15.

[2] Taraṅga, vii, 231-233, 245, 322 f.

(931-954)[1] for instance, is in part co-eval with that of his son Mahendrapāla II (946 A.D.),[2] and Mahendra's brother or cousin Devapāla (948-49).[3] It is easy to suggest that we have to do with two different Vināyakas, one flourishing before Mahendrapāla II, and the other after Devapāla. But anything in the nature of a proof is not forthcoming, and conjectural duplication of kings in such cases is not always a satisfactory solution of the problem, specially in view of the fact that simultaneous rule of father and son,[4] or of uncle and nephew,[5] and the abdication of a father in favour of his son,[6] and resumption of control on

[1] Majumdār, *Gurjara Pratihāras*, pp. 54 (esp. the footnote) and 62.

[2] *Ep. Ind.*, xiv, p. 176 f.

[3] Kielhorn, *Northern Ins.*, No. 31 ; *Ep. Ind.*, i. 173. xiv. 179-180.

[4] *Camb. Hist. Ind.*, Vol. I, 572-573; Smith, *EHI*[4], p. 486 (Conjoint Reign of Chola Kings).

[5] *Camb. Hist. Ind.*, Vol. I, 574, 578.

[6] *Cf.* the case of Ananta in the Rāja-taraṅgiṇī, and of Vigrahapāla :—

> Tapo mamāstu rājyaṁ te
> dvābhyām uktam idaṁ dvayoḥ
> yasmin Vigrahapālena
> Sagareṇa Bhagīrathe.
>
> (Bhāgalpur Plate.)

account of the son's incapacity,[1] or other reason, are not rare phenomena in Ancient Indian History.

[1] *Cf.* the case of Kalasa in the Rājataraṅgiṇī. In the *Catalogue of the Coins of the Andhra Dynasty, the Western Kshatrapas, etc.*, p. cxxiv ff., Rapson points out that the satrap Jīvadāman reigned twice, and the two reigns are separated by a long interval during which his uncle Rudrasiṁha I appears twice as Kshatrapa and Mahākshatrapa.

CHAPTER X

Epigraphic Notes

1. *Pārijāta and Govardhana.*

The Daulatābād plates of the Rāshṭrakūṭa Saṅkaragaṇa [1] after referring to Kṛishṇarāja I say: "His son was king Govinda-rāja who like Hari snatched away the glory of Śrî Pārijāta and supported Govardhana." The Purāṇic allusion is clear enough. But the references in the case of king Govinda are not so certain. Professor D. R. Bhandarkar, who edited the plates, has suggested the identification of Govardhana with the province of the same name mentioned in several Nāsik cave inscriptions. But the identification of Pārijāta is yet uncertain. I propose to identify it with Pārichāta (=Pāriyātra=the Western Vindhya [2]) mentioned in the Nāsik praśasti of Gautamîputra Sātakarṇi.[3] The change of 'j' into 'ch' is not unusual in southern India. For instance, the Western Gaṅga king 'Rājamalla' was also called 'Rāchamalla.' [4]

1 *Epigraphia Indica*, ix, p. 193.

2 Pārijāta may also refer to the 'Pāriyātra country mentioned by Bāṇa (Cowell and Thomas, Harshacharita, pp. 210-211) and Yuan Chwang.

3 *Ep. Ind.*, viii, p. 60.

4 Rice, *Mysore and Coorg from the Inscriptions*, p. 42.

2. *Supratishṭhāhāra.*

This name occurs in the Poona plates of the Vākāṭaka Queen Prabhāvatî-guptā, edited by Prof. Pāṭhak and Mr. Dikshit.[1] The editors do not make any suggestion regarding the identification of the place. In the Kathā-sarit-sāgara[2] mention is made of a city named Supratishṭhita in Pratishṭhāna (modern Paiṭhaṇ), which was the ancestral home of Guṇāḍhya. There can be no doubt that Supratishṭhāhāra was the district (āhāra) round the city of Supratishṭha or Supratishṭhita. The inclusion of this district within the Vākāṭaka territory proves that the Vākāṭakas were not merely a dynasty of Berar, but ruled over a considerable part of Mahārāshṭra. As the dynasty lasted from about A.D. 300 to 500,[3] it is no longer correct to say that "for some three centuries after the extinction of the Andhra dynasty, we have no specific information about the dynasties that ruled over the country," *i.e.*, Mahārāshṭra.

3. *Vīra and Vardhana.*

The Deopārā inscription[4] records that Vijayasena impetuously assailed the lord of Gauḍa, put

1 *Ep. Ind.*, xv, p. 39.

2 Tawney's translation, p. 32.

3 V. A. Smith, "The Vākāṭaka Dynasty of Berar," *JRAS*, 1914, pp. 317-328.

4 *Ep. Ind.*, i, pp. 307-311.

down the prince of Kāmarūpa, defeated Kaliṅga and imprisoned four kings, namely, Nānya, Vîra, Rāghava and Vardhana. Nānya has been correctly identified with Nānyadeva of Tirhut, who lived in A.D. 1097 and afterwards established the Karṇāṭaka dynasty in the valley of Nepāl. Rāghava is the Kaliṅga prince of that name, who reigned about A.D. 1156.[1] Vîra and Vardhana have, however, not been satisfactorily identified. Dr. Smith suggests that Vîra was a Rājā of Kāmarūpa. Unfortunately the evidence of Sandhyākara Nandî's *Rāma-charita* has not been utilised in this connection. In the long list of princes who helped Rāmapāla to recover Varendrî we find the following names :—

1. Vîraguṇa of Kōtāṭavî.[2]
2. Vardhana of Kauśāmbî.
3. Vijaya-rāja of Nidrāvala.

Let us try to ascertain the dates of these princes. We learn from the Tirumalai Rock Inscription[3] of Rājendra Chola I that Mahîpāla I of Bengal was reigning in or about A.D. 1025. The Sārnāth inscription gives a date for him in A.D. 1026.[4] His son Nayapāla ruled for at least 15

[1] V. A. Smith, *The Early History of India*, 1914, p. 419.

[2] *Mem. ASB*, iii, pp. 36-37.

[3] *Ep. Ind.*, xi, pp. 229-232.

[4] Smith, *Early History of India*, 1914, p. 399.

years as we know from the Kṛishṇa-dvārikā temple inscription.[1] Nayapāla's son Vigrahapāla III could not, therefore, have come to the throne before A.D. 1026+15=A.D. 1041. He ruled for at least 13 years (see the Āmagāchhi grant[2]), *i.e.*, up to at least A.D. 1054. After him came his sons Mahîpāla II and Śūrapāla II, and the Kaivartas Divvoka, Rudoka and Bhîma, and finally Rāmapāla who ruled for at least 42 years.[3] It is obvious that Rāmapāla reigned towards the close of the eleventh century and early in the twelfth century. The princes Vîra, Vardhana and Vijaya who helped him must have flourished about the same time.

We learn from the Naihāṭî grant[4] of Ballāla-sena that his ancestors were ruling in South-West Bengal (Rāḍhā)[5] long before the establishment of their paramount sovereignty by Vijaya-sena's victory over the (Pāla) king of Gauḍa. We know further from the Deopārā inscription that Vijaya-sena was a contemporary of Nānyadeva. The latter

1 *Gauḍa-lekha-mālā*, p. 115.

2 *Op. cit.*, p. 122.

3 *Mem. ASB*, v, p. 92.

4 *Ep. Ind.*, xiv, pp. 156-63.

5 *Prauḍhāṁ Rāḍhām-akalitacharair-bhūshayanto'-nubhāvaiḥ*. The association of the Karṇāṭas—the race to which the Senas belonged—with the sovereigns of Bengal can be traced back to the time of Devapāla (*cf.* the Monghyr Plate).

flourished about A.D. 1097. There can be no objection in identifying him with Vijaya-rāja of the *Rāma-charita* who lived about the same time and ruled over a principality in the Gauḍa empire.[1] If this identification be correct, then Vîra and Vardhana must be Vîraguṇa of Kōṭāṭavî and Vardhana of Kauśāmbî. It seems reasonable to conclude that during the weak rule of the sons of Rāmapāla, the kinglets of the Gauḍa Empire who helped Rāmapāla to regain his throne, engaged in a struggle for supremacy[2] in the course of which Vîra, Vardhana, the rājā of Kāmarūpa and the lord of Gauḍa himself were worsted, and Vijayasena established the supremacy of his own family.

The conqueror's authority was probably next challenged by Nānya and Rāghava, the rulers of the neighbouring kingdoms of Mithilā and Kaliṅga,[3] who were also defeated and imprisoned.

[1] The identification was first suggested by Mr. N. N. Basu.

[2] The Kamauli grant of Vaidyadeva, minister and general of Kumārapāla, son and successor of Rāmapāla, refers to wars and rebellions in South Bengal and Kāmarūpa (see *Gauḍalekhamālā*, p. 128, *et seq.*). Vijayasena's principality lay in south-west Bengal. Vîraguṇa's principality also lay in the south, *cf. Mem. ASB*, v, p. 89.

[3] Among other rivals was probably Vikramāṅka (=Sāhasāṅka) of Kalyāṇa (1076-*c.* 1127) as the epithet *Vikrama-tiraskṛita-Sāhasāṅka* of the Naihāṭi grant seems to suggest.

CHAPTER XI

The Lakshmaṇa-sena Era

The universal belief among scholars is that the Lakshmaṇa-sena Era originated with the Sena Dynasty of Bengal. According to one group of scholars[1] the era marks the accession of king Lakshmaṇa-sena of Bengal, son of Ballāla-sena (Ballāl Sen), who is represented by Dhoyi as ruling in the city of Vijayapura. Professor Kielhorn has proved that the first day of the era was October 7, A.D. 1119, and the first current year, as reckoned from the era, was A.D. 1119-20. Consequently Lakshmaṇa-sena must have ascended the throne in A.D. 1119, and died before 1170, as an inscription of the year 51 of the era speaks of his reign as *atīta* or past.

According to another group of scholars[2] the era commemorates the accession or coronation of a predecessor of king Lakshmaṇa-sena of Bengal who himself ruled in the last quarter of the twelfth century A.D.

[1] *E.g.*, Kielhorn, *Indian Antiquary*, Vol. XIX, p. 2 ; R. D. Banerji, *J. & P. A. S. B.*, Vol. IX, 1913, p. 273, *et seq.*; S. Kumār, *Ind. Ant.*, 1913, p. 188.

[2] *E.g.*, M. Chakravarti, *J. & P. A. S. B.* (N.S.), Vol. I (1905), p. 48, *et seq.*; V. A. Smith, *The Early History of India*, Third Edition, p. 418.

Both the views are open to serious objections. The first theory is opposed not only to the evidence of certain passages of the *Dāna-sāgara* and the *Adbhuta-sāgara*, two works attributed to king Ballāla-sena (Ballāl Sen), the father of Lakshmaṇa-sena, but also to the testimony of the *Ṭabaqāt-i-Nāṣirī* which was written by Minhāj-i-Sirāj in A.H. 658 (A.D. 1260).

Two manuscripts of the *Dāna-sāgara* contain the following passage : [1]

> nikhila-chakra-tilaka śrîmad-Ballālasenena pūrṇe
> śaśi-navadaśamite Śakavarshe Dānasāgaro rachitaḥ.

One of these manuscripts is in the India Office collection and in this the date is given in numerical figures also. The other is in the possession of Babu Nagendra Nāth Basu. This manuscript contains two more verses elucidating the date.

A manuscript of the *Adbhuta-sāgara* now in the collection of the Bombay Government, contains the following verse :—

> śāke khanavakhendvabde ārebhe'dbhuta-sāgaram
> Gauḍendra-kuñjarālāna-stambhabāhur mahîpatiḥ.

[1] *J. & P. A. S. B.* (New Series), Vol. IX, 1913, p. 274.

The agreement of the dates from two different works seems to prove beyond doubt that Ballāla-sena (Ballāl Sen), father of Lakshmaṇa-sena, was alive in the Śaka years 1090-91, *i.e.*, A.D. 1168-69. Consequently it has to be admitted that Lakshmaṇa-sena ascended the throne, not in the year A.D. 1119, but after A.D. 1169.

The passages of the *Dāna-sāgara* and the *Adbhuta-sāgara* quoted above have been rejected as late interpolations by Mr. R. D. Banerji.[1] The evidence of Minhāj-i Sirāj cannot, however, be dismissed so summarily. According to the narrative contained in the *Tabaqāt-i-Nāṣirî*, written by Minhāj in A.H. 658 (A.D. 1260), Rāe Lakhmaniya (Rājā Lakshmaṇa) was ruling in Bengal at the time of the Nudîah raid of Muhammad bin Bakhtyār, which took place after A.H. 589 and "some years" before A.H. 601, *i.e.*, between A.D. 1193 and 1205.[2]

The second theory seeks to reconcile the dates of Ballāla-sena (Ballāl Sen) and Lakshmaṇa-sena given in the *Dāna-sāgara*, the *Adbhuta-sāgara*, and the *Tabaqāt-i-Nāṣirî*, with the initial date of the Lakshmaṇa-sena Era, as determined by Kielhorn, by attributing the establishment of the era to a predecessor of Lakshmaṇa. But this theory ignores the fact that the era of A.D. 1119

[1] *J. & P.A.S.B.* (New Series), Vol. IX, 1913, p. 275.

[2] Smith, *The Early History of India*, Third Edition, pp. 416-17.

is distinctly called *Lakshmaṇābda* and *Lakshmaṇa-sena varsha* in several ancient manuscripts discovered by Paṇḍit Haraprasād Sastrî.[1] Again, it does not satisfactorily explain why the word *atîta* is used in reference to the *rājya* of Lakshmaṇa-sena in the Bodh-Gayā inscription of the year 51 (A.D. 1170).

There is another important fact which has been ignored by both the groups of scholars mentioned above. The Sena kings of Bengal never use the era which they are said to have established. All the inscriptions of this dynasty hitherto discovered are dated in regnal years. Even the records of Viśvarūpa-sena and Keśava-sena, the two sons of Lakshmaṇa-sena, form no exception. The copper-plate inscription of Vijaya-sena is dated in the year 31 (or 62).[2] The Naihāṭî grant of Ballāla-sena is dated in the year 11.[3] The Tarpaṇadîghi and Ānulia grants, and the Dacca Chaṇḍî image inscription of the time of Lakshmaṇa-sena, are dated in the years 2 and 3.[4] The Madanapāḍa

[1] *J. & P.A.S.B.* (New Series), Vol. II, 1906, p. 16; *cf.* '*A Catalogue of Palm-leaf and Selected Paper Manuscripts belonging to the Darbar Library, Nepal*, pp. 33, 51.

[2] R. D. Banerji, *Bāṅgālāra Itihāsa*, pp. 290-91; Majumdār, *Inscriptions of Bengal*, 59.

[3] R. D. Banerji, *Epigraphia Indica*, Vol. XIV, pp. 156-163.

[4] R. D. Banerji, *Bāṅgālāra Itihāsa*, pp. 297-98; Majumdār, *Inscriptions of Bengal*, 100.

grant of Viśvarūpa-sena is dated in the year 14. The Edilpur grant of Keśava-sena is dated in the year 3.[1] These dates do not suggest a continuous reckoning. A glance at them is sufficient to show that they are the regnal years of the reigning monarchs, and not years of the Lakshmaṇa-sena Era.[2]

On the contrary we find that the era is used in Bihār and is associated with a line of Sena kings who are described as lords of Pîṭhî. The Jānîbighā inscription records the grant of a village to the Vajrāsana for the residence of the Ceylonese monk, Maṅgalasvāmin, by king Jayasena, the lord of Pîṭhî, son of Buddhasena.[3] The inscription bears the date, the year 83 of the Lakshmaṇa-sena Era, the 15th day of the bright half of the month of Kārttika. Mr. Jayaswal has pointed out that the commentator of the Rāma-charita explains the word *Pîṭhî-pati* (lord of Pîthî) by *Magadhādhipa.*[4] Consequently Jayasena was a king of South Bihār.

[1] R. D. Banerji, *Bāṅgālāra Itihāsa*, p. 323, *J.A.S.B.*, lxv, Part I, p. 15; *J.A.S.B.*, vii, Part I, p. 46; and *J. & P.A.S.B.* (New Series), x, 104.

[2] When the Senas of Bengal (or their court *Pundits*) do use an era, as in the *Dānasāgara*, the *Adbhuta-sāgara* and the *Saduktikarṇāmṛita* it is the Saka Era, and not the Lakshmaṇa Sena Era, that is so used.

[3] N. G. Majumdār, Patna Museum Inscription of Jayasena, *Indian Antiquary*, Vol. XLVIII, 1919, p. 47.

[4] *J.B.O.R.S.*, Vol. IV, p. 267; *cf.* also *Bāṅgālāra Itihāsa*, p. 257, n (43).

Another epigraph discovered at Bodh-Gayā [1] mentions Buddhasena, father of Jayasena, describes him as *Pīṭhī-pati*, and represents him as a contemporary of Aśokachalla, king of a Himālayan district, two of whose inscriptions found at Bodh-Gayā bear the dates 51 and 74 of the Lakshmaṇa-sena Era.[2]

In his *Catalogue of Palm-leaf and Selected Paper Manuscripts belonging to the Darbar Library, Nepal*, Paṇḍit Haraprasād Śāstrî notices some fifty-seven manuscripts which contain colophons dated in the Lakshmaṇa Saṁvat, ranging from the year 91 (in the manuscript No. 400, p. 15) to the year 558 (No. 1076 [ঞ], p. 31). Most of these manuscripts are written in Maithila (Northern Bihāri) characters and the earliest dates (91 and 116) are found in the Maithila manuscripts. The evidence of these records and that of the Bodh-Gayā and the Jānîbighā inscriptions leaves no room for doubt that the earliest use of the Lakshmaṇa-sena Era was confined to the province of Bihār.

In his note on "Trikūṭa and the so-called Kalachuri or Chedi Era," [3] Dr. Fleet observes: "Any era may be introduced into a country in

[1] *Indian Antiquary*, Vol. XLVIII, 1919, p. 45.

[2] Kielhorn, 'A List of the Inscriptions of Northern India'; Ins. Nos. 576 and 577, *Epigraphia Indica*, Vol. V, Appendix, p. 79.

[3] *J.R.A.S.*, 1905, p. 568.

which it was not founded. But no era can have been founded in a country in which it was never used." We have seen that the Lakshmaṇa-sena Era was never used in Bengal by its alleged founders, the Sena kings of Vijayapura. The earliest use of it was confined to Bihār where we have epigraphic evidence of the existence of a line of Sena kings who actually use the era. It is fair to conclude from this that the origin of the Lakshmaṇa-sena Era is to be sought not in the Sena dynasty of Vijayapura (Bengal) but in the Sena dynasty of Pîṭhî (Bihār). King Jayasena was ruling in the year 83 of this era. His father, king Buddhasena, was a contemporary of Aśokachalla who lived in the years 51 and 74 of this era. The parts of the Bodh-Gayā and Jānîbighā inscriptions which contain the dates 51, 74 and 83 run as follows[1] :—

Śrīmal-Lakhvana (kshmaṇa)-senasy
=ātītarājye Saṁ 51.
Śrīmal-Lakshmaṇa-sena-deva-pādānām
=atītarājye Saṁ 74.
Lakshmaṇa-senasy=ātītarājye Saṁ 83.

The most important point in these dates is the use of the word *atīta*. Professor Kielhorn remarks: "During the reign of Lakshmaṇa-sena the years of

[1] *Indian Antiquary*, Vol. XLVIII, 1919, p. 171. *Epigraphia Indica*, Vol. XII, pp. 29-30.

his reign would be described as *Srīmal-Lakshmaṇa-sena-devapādānāṁ rājye* (or *pravardhamāna-vijaya-rājye*) *Saṁvat*, after his death the phrase would be retained, but *atîta* prefixed to the word *rājye*, to show that, although the years were still counted from the commencement of the reign of Lakshmaṇa-sena, that reign itself was a thing of the past." [1] The founder of the Lakshmaṇa-sena Era whose reign was a thing of the past in the year 51 (=A.D. 1170) cannot be identified with Lakshmaṇa-sena of Bengal, the son and successor of the author of the *Dāna-sāgara* and the *Adbhuta-sāgara*, who was driven out of Nūdîah by Muhammad bin Bakhtyār at some date subsequent to the taking of Delhi by the Muhammadans in A.H. 589, which is practically equivalent to A.D. 1193, and prior to Muhammad's expedition into the hills of the N.E. frontier, called Tibbat (Tibet) by the author of the *Tabaqāt-i-Nāṣirî*, which took place in A.H. 601 (August 1204-August 1205).

If the founder of the Lakshmaṇa-sena Era was not identical with king Lakshmaṇa-sena of Bengal, he must have been the founder of the Sena dynasty of Pîṭhî. This explains why his reckoning is perpetuated by king Jayasena of Pîṭhî, but

[1] *Indian Antiquary*, Vol. XIX, p. 2. The analogy of the Gayā Inscription of Govinda-pāla (V. 1232) suggests that, like *gatarājya* of that record, *atîta-rājya* can have no reference to any change resulting from the Muslim conquest.

is never used by any Sena king of Bengal, not even by Viśvarūpa-sena and Keśava-sena, the sons and immediate successors of king Lakshmaṇa of Bengal. This also explains why the era is used in the records of Bodh-Gayā and Mithilā from the first century of its existence, but never appears in a Bengali manuscript till 171 years had elapsed from the time of the founder. The era is not connected with a Gauḍa king till the year 432.

PART IV

EPIC AND GEOGRAPHICAL STUDIES (IN BENGALI)

PART IV

Epic and Geographical Studies (in Bengali)

CHAPTER XII

মহাভারত ও বুদ্ধচরিত

ভারতবর্ষের যে কয়েকজন পুরুষশ্রেষ্ঠ প্রাচীন এবং আধুনিক ধর্ম্ম-সম্প্রদায়ের উপাস্য দেবতারূপে পূজিত হইয়াছেন বা হইতেছেন তন্মধ্যে রঘুকুলভূষণ শ্রীরামচন্দ্র, চন্দ্রবংশোদ্ভব বাসুদেবার্জ্জুন এবং শাক্যকুল-চূড়ামণি গৌতম বুদ্ধই প্রধান। ইঁহাদের জীবনের ঘটনাবলীকে কেন্দ্র করিয়াই প্রাচীন ভারতের সর্ব্বশ্রেষ্ঠ মহাকাব্যগুলি গড়িয়া উঠিয়াছে। রামচরিত্র-মাহাত্ম্যই মহর্ষি বাল্মীকি-বিরচিত রামায়ণ ও কবিকুলশ্রেষ্ঠ কালিদাস-প্রণীত রঘুবংশের প্রধান প্রতিপাদ্য বিষয়। মহর্ষি কৃষ্ণদ্বৈপায়ন ও মহাকবি ভারবি বাসুদেবার্জ্জুনের বিচিত্র চরিত-কথা অবলম্বন করিয়াই মহাভারত ও কিরাতার্জ্জুনীয় গ্রন্থ রচনা করিয়াছেন। সিদ্ধার্থ-গৌতমের অপূর্ব্ব জীবন-কাহিনীই বৌদ্ধ পণ্ডিত অশ্বঘোষকে তাঁহার অমর গ্রন্থ বুদ্ধচরিত লিখিতে অনুপ্রাণিত করিয়াছিল। উল্লিখিত মহাকাব্যগুলি স্বতন্ত্র ভাবে গড়িয়া উঠে নাই। উহাদের মধ্যে প্রাচীনতম কাব্যগুলির প্রভাব অপেক্ষাকৃত আধুনিক গ্রন্থগুলির উপর স্পষ্ট বিদ্যমান দেখিতে পাওয়া যায়। রামায়ণ ও মহাভারতের পরস্পর সম্বন্ধ স্থানান্তরে আলোচনা করিয়াছি, বুদ্ধচরিতে মহাভারত আখ্যানের প্রভাব প্রদর্শন করা বর্ত্তমান প্রবন্ধের আলোচ্য বিষয়।

মহাভারতের প্রভাব ভারতবর্ষের সর্ব্বত্র দৃষ্ট হয়। কাশীদাস প্রভৃতি বঙ্গ-কবিগণের অনুগ্রহে ভারতোক্ত ঘটনাবলী বঙ্গের ঘরে ঘরে সুপরিচিত। কিন্তু এক সময়ে সুদূর গন্ধারের বৌদ্ধ নরপতিগণের সভাসদ্‌গণও যে ইহার চর্চ্চা করিতেন তাহা বুদ্ধচরিত-পাঠে স্পষ্টই প্রতীতি হয়। পঞ্জাবের পশ্চিমোত্তরে সিন্ধু নদের উভয় পার্শ্বে অবস্থিত ভূখণ্ডই প্রাচীন কালে গন্ধার বলিয়া অভিহিত হইত। খৃষ্টীয় প্রথম শতাব্দে এই দেশ মধ্য-এশিয়াবাসী কুষানগণ কর্ত্তৃক বিজিত হয়। কুষানবংশীয় সর্ব্বশ্রেষ্ঠ নরপতি রাজাধিরাজ দেবপুত্র কনিষ্ক গন্ধারদেশান্তর্গত পুরুষপুর (বর্ত্তমান পেশাওয়ার) নগরে শাসনদণ্ড পরিচালন করিতেন। তিনি বৌদ্ধ ধর্ম্মাবলম্বী ছিলেন এবং বৌদ্ধ পণ্ডিত অশ্বঘোষ তাঁহার রাজসভা অলঙ্কৃত করিতেন বলিয়া বহু গ্রন্থে লিখিত আছে। অশ্বঘোষই বুদ্ধচরিত মহাকাব্যের রচয়িতা। বৌদ্ধ নরপতির বৌদ্ধ সভাসদ্‌রচিত বুদ্ধচরিতে মহাভারতের প্রভাব অনেকের নিকটই বিস্ময়কর বলিয়া বোধ হইবে। কিন্তু অশ্বঘোষ বাস্তবিকই যে মহাভারতের, বিশেষতঃ আদিপর্ব্বের, ঘটনাবলীর সহিত সুপরিচিত ছিলেন এ বিষয়ে সন্দেহের লেশমাত্র কারণ নাই।

ইতিহাস-পাঠকমাত্রই অবগত আছেন যে কুমার সিদ্ধার্থের মন ঐহিক সুখের প্রতি বীতরাগ ছিল; পিতা শুদ্ধোধন বিলাসব্যসনে বীতশ্রদ্ধ পুত্রের মন "কামজ সুখের" প্রতি আকৃষ্ট করিবার জন্য প্রভূত চেষ্টা করিয়াছিলেন। এই চেষ্টায় তাঁহার প্রধান সহায় ছিল পুরোহিত-পুত্র-উদায়ী। উদায়ী-প্রমুখ শুদ্ধোদন-নিয়োজিত অমাত্যবর্গ নানা প্রকারে কুমারের মন ভুলাইতে প্রয়াস পাইয়াছিলেন। তাঁহারা পূর্ব্ববর্ত্তী রাজা

ও মুনিগণের বিবরণ উল্লেখ করিয়া বলিতেন যে "কুমার, এতাদৃশ বিখ্যাত নরবরগণও যখন বিষয়সুখে অনাসক্ত ছিলেন না তখন আপনিই বা কেন সংসার-ত্যাগী হইয়া পিতার মনে সন্তাপ জন্মাইতেছেন?" কুমারকে পিতার আজ্ঞাকারী এবং তাঁহার মন বিলাসব্যসনে আসক্ত করিবার নিমিত্ত যে সকল দৃষ্টান্ত বুদ্ধচরিতে প্রদর্শিত হইয়াছে তাহার অনেকগুলি মহাভারতের আদিপর্ব্বে দেখিতে পাওয়া যায়।

কালীং চৈব পুরা কন্যাং জলপ্রভবসংভবাম্।
জগাম যমুনাতীরে জাতরাগঃ পরাশরঃ ॥
স্ত্রীসংসর্গং বিনাশান্তং পাংডুর্জ্ঞাত্বাপি কৌরবঃ।
মাদ্রীরূপ-গুণাক্ষিপ্তঃ সিষেবে কামজং সুখম্ ॥
উতথ্যস্য চ ভার্য্যায়াং মমতায়াং মহাতপাঃ।
মারুত্যাং জনয়ামাস ভরদ্বাজং বৃহস্পতিঃ ॥

মহাকবি অশ্বঘোষ কেবল আদিপর্ব্ব-বর্ণিত রাজা ও ঋষিগণের বিলাসলীলার সহিত যে শুধু পরিচিত ছিলেন তাহা নহে, নিম্নলিখিত শ্লোকগুলিতে তিনি ভীষ্মের অসাধারণ পিতৃভক্তি ও রণপাণ্ডিত্য, পাণ্ডবগণের শৌর্য্যবীর্য্য ও শূরবংশধর বাসুদেব-কৃষ্ণের অনন্যসাধারণ কার্য্যাবলীর পরিচয় প্রদান করিয়াছেন।—

ভীষ্মেণ গংগোদরসংভবেন
রামেণ রামেণ চ ভার্গবেণ
শ্রুত্বা কৃতং কর্ম্ম পিতুঃ প্রিয়ার্থং
পিতুস্তমপ্যর্হসি কর্ত্তুমিষ্টম্ ॥

উগ্রায়ুধশ্চোগ্রধৃতায়ুধোঽপি
যেষাং কৃতে মৃত্যুমবাপ ভীষ্মাৎ ॥
সপাংডবং পাংডবতুল্যবীর্য্যঃ
শৈলোত্তমং শৈলসমানবর্ষ্ম
মৌলিধরঃ সিংহগতির্নৃসিংহ-
শ্চলৎসটঃ সিংহ ইবারুরোহ ॥
আচার্য্যকং যোগবিধৌ দ্বিজানাং
অপ্রাপ্তমন্যৈর্জনকো জগাম
খ্যাতানি কর্ম্মাণি চ যানি শৌরেঃ
শূরাদয়স্তেষ্ববলা বভূবুঃ ॥

উল্লিখিত শ্লোকগুলি পাঠ করিলে স্পষ্টই প্রতীতি হয় যে বুদ্ধচরিত-রচয়িতা অশ্বঘোষের পাণ্ডিত্য শুধু বৌদ্ধ শাস্ত্রেই সীমাবদ্ধ ছিল না, তিনি অবৌদ্ধ-প্রণীত মহাভারত গ্রন্থও যত্নসহকারে অধ্যয়ন করিয়াছিলেন। প্রাচীন ভারতবর্ষীয় মনীষিগণ যে ধর্ম্মনির্ব্বিশেষে বিদ্যাচর্চ্চা করিতেন ইহা তাহার এক প্রকৃষ্ট উদাহরণ।

এই আখ্যানটী খিল-হরিবংশপর্ব্বের বিংশোঽধ্যায়ে দেখিতে পাওয়া যায়। সুতরাং হরিবংশপর্ব্বও সম্ভবতঃ বুদ্ধচরিতের পূর্ব্ববর্ত্তী।

CHAPTER XIII

মহাভারত ও মধ্যমব্যায়োগ

ত্রিবান্দ্রাম-নিবাসী বিশ্ববিশ্রুত পণ্ডিত মহামহোপাধ্যায় গণপতি শাস্ত্রীর উদ্যম ও অনুসন্ধিৎসার ফলে যে কয়খানি বিলুপ্তপ্রায় প্রাচীন সংস্কৃত নাট্যগ্রন্থ সম্প্রতি আবিষ্কৃত ও প্রকাশিত হইয়াছে মধ্যমব্যায়োগ তাহাদের অন্যতম। এই গ্রন্থখানি এবং ইহার সংশ্লিষ্ট অন্যান্য নাটক মহাকবি ভাস-প্রণীত কিনা এবং এগুলি কোন্ শতাব্দীতে রচিত হইয়াছে এই সকল জটিল প্রশ্নের মীমাংসা বর্ত্তমান প্রবন্ধের বিষয়ীভূত নহে। ভারতবর্ষ ও শ্বেতবর্ষের মনীষিগণ ঐ সকল তথ্য নিরূপণের জন্য বহু পুস্তক ও প্রবন্ধ রচনা করিয়া যশস্বী হইয়াছেন। কিন্তু নাটক-গুলির আখ্যান-ভাগ-সম্বন্ধে পর্য্যাপ্ত আলোচনা হইয়াছে বলিয়া মনে হয় না। অনেকগুলি গল্প রামায়ণ ও মহাভারতের অক্ষয় ভাণ্ডার হইতে গৃহীত। কিন্তু প্রচলিত রামায়ণ ও ভারতী-কথার সহিত এই সকল আখ্যানের বিস্তর প্রভেদ পরিদৃষ্ট হয়। এই পার্থক্য বিশেষ ভাবে লক্ষ্য করিবার যোগ্য, কারণ উহা দ্বারা মহর্ষি বাল্মীকি ও কৃষ্ণদ্বৈপায়ন-ব্যাসপ্রোক্ত মহাগ্রন্থ-দ্বয়ের উপচয় ও পরিণতির ইতিহাস অনেকখানি সুস্পষ্ট হইবে বলিয়া আশা করা যায়। এই সম্বন্ধে বিস্তৃত আলোচনা করিতে গেলে একখানি বৃহৎ গ্রন্থ লিখিতে হয়। যাঁহারা প্রাচীন বৈয়াসকী সংহিতার পরিবর্ত্তন, পরিবর্দ্ধন ও ক্রমবিকাশের ইতিহাস-সঙ্কলনে যত্নবান্ তাঁহারা শাস্ত্রী-প্রকাশিত মধ্যমব্যায়োগ-নামধেয় নাটকখানি হইতে কোন সাহায্য প্রাপ্ত হইতে পারেন

কিনা সেই বিষয়ে তুই একটি কথা বলাই এই ক্ষুদ্র প্রবন্ধের উদ্দেশ্য।

মধ্যম পাণ্ডব ভীমসেন এবং তৎপুত্র হিড়িম্বা-তনয় রাক্ষসবীর ঘটোৎকচের কাহিনী অবলম্বনে মধ্যমব্যায়োগ লিখিত। একদা ঘটোৎকচ মাতার আহারের নিমিত্ত তাহারই আজ্ঞায় মনুষ্য-শিকারের অন্বেষণ করিতে করিতে সুতত্রয়কলত্র-পরিবৃত ব্রাহ্মণ কেশবদাসের পশ্চাদ্ধাবন করিয়াছিলেন। তিনি কেশবদাসের মধ্যম পুত্রকে বলপূর্ব্বক গ্রহণ করিবার জন্য উদ্যত হইলে তাঁহার আহ্বানধ্বনি শুনিয়া অদূরে ব্যায়ামনিরত ভীমসেন সেখানে উপস্থিত হইলেন এবং স্ত্রীপুত্রসহ দ্বিজসত্তম কেশবদাসকে মোচন করিবার জন্য হিড়িম্বা-নন্দনকে অনুজ্ঞা করিলেন। ঘটোৎকচ অস্বীকৃত হইলে পিতাপুত্রে যুদ্ধ হয়, পরে ব্রাহ্মণ-কুমারের পরিবর্ত্তে স্বয়ং ভীমসেন হিড়িম্বা-সকাশে গমন করিতে স্বীকৃত হইলেন। অনন্তর হিড়িম্বা-তনয় মাতার নিকট বৃকোদরের প্রকৃত পরিচয় পাইলে পিতাপুত্রে মিলন হয়। এই গল্পটির সহিত প্রচলিত মহাভারতের আখ্যান-ভাগের সম্বন্ধ বিচার করিতে হইলে প্রচলিত মহাভারত ব্যতীত অপর কোনও ভারত-সংহিতা ছিল কিনা সে সম্বন্ধে সংক্ষিপ্ত আলোচনা কর্ত্তব্য।

যে মহাকাব্য বর্ত্তমান সময়ে মহর্ষি কৃষ্ণদ্বৈপায়ন-ব্যাস-প্রণীত মহাভারত বলিয়া প্রচলিত, উহা যে লক্ষ-শ্লোকাত্মক তাহা সকলেই অবগত আছেন।

ইদং শতসহস্রন্তু লোকানাং পুণ্যকর্ম্মণাম্।
উপাখ্যানৈঃ সহ জ্ঞেয়মাদ্যং ভারতমুত্তমম্। ১।১।১০১

২১৪ গুপ্তাব্দে (খৃঃ ৫৩৩-৩৪) উৎকীর্ণ মহারাজ সর্ব্বনাথের খোহ্‌লিপিতেও পরমর্ষি পরাশর-সুত বেদব্যাস-রচিত মহাভারত

গ্রন্থ শতসাহস্রী সংহিতা বলিয়া নির্ণীত হইয়াছে। কিন্তু অতি পূর্ব্বকালে এই মহাগ্রন্থের আয়তন যে অপেক্ষাকৃত ক্ষুদ্র ছিল ইহার অনেক প্রমাণ পাওয়া যায়।

আদিম মহাভারত অশ্বঘোষ, পতঞ্জলি, এমন কি পাণিনি ও আশ্বলায়নেরও পূর্ব্ববর্ত্তী। কিন্তু বর্ত্তমান গ্রন্থে এমন অনেক কথা আছে যাহা পাণিনির পূর্ব্ববর্ত্তী বলিয়া কোন ক্রমেই মনে করা যাইতে পারে না। প্রচলিত মহাভারতের আদি ও স্বর্গারোহণপর্ব্বে হরিবংশ ও অষ্টাদশ পুরাণের উল্লেখ দৃষ্ট হয়—

> হরিবংশস্ততঃ পর্ব্ব পুরাণং খিলসংজ্ঞিতম্।
> বিষ্ণুপর্ব্ব শিশোশ্চর্য্যা বিষ্ণোঃ কংসবধস্তথা।
> ভবিষ্যং পর্ব্ব চাপ্যুক্তং খিলেষ্বেবাদ্ভুতং মহৎ। ১।২।৮২-৮৩
>
> *　　*　　*　　*
>
> হরিবংশ-সমাপ্তৌ তু সহস্রং ভোজয়েদ্দ্বিজান্। ১৮।৬।৭১
>
> *　　*　　*　　*
>
> অষ্টাদশ-পুরাণানাং শ্রবণাদ্ যৎ ফলং ভবেৎ
> তৎফলং সমবাপ্নোতি বৈষ্ণবো নাত্র সংশয়ঃ। ১৮।৬।৯৭

বনপর্ব্বে মার্কণ্ডেয়-সমস্যা-পর্ব্বাধ্যায়ে মাৎস্যকপুরাণ ও বায়ুপুরাণের নামোল্লেখ আছে এবং বায়ুপুরাণে যে অতীত এবং অনাগত উভয়বিধ ঘটনা লিখিত আছে উহার স্পষ্ট উল্লেখ আছে—

> সর্ব্বাঃ প্রজা মনুঃ সাক্ষাদ্ যথাবস্তুরতর্ষভ।
> ইত্যেতম্মাৎস্যকং নাম পুরাণং পরিকীর্ত্তিতম্। ৩।১৮৭।৫৭
>
> *　　*　　*　　*
>
> এতত্তে সর্ব্বমাখ্যাতমতীতানাগতং ময়া।
> বায়ুপ্রোক্তমনুস্মৃত্য পুরাণমৃষিসংস্তুতম্। ৩।১৯১।১৬

পাণিনি ও আশ্বলায়নের পূর্ব্বে যে হরিবংশ এবং অতীত ও অনাগত রাজগণের কাহিনীপূর্ণ বায়ু এবং মৎস্যপ্রমুখ অষ্টাদশ পুরাণ রচিত হইয়াছিল—ইহা বোধ হয় কেহই বলিবেন না। অবশ্য প্রাচীন বৈদিক সাহিত্যে পুরাণের উল্লেখ নাই এমন কথা বলা যায় না, কিন্তু ঐ পুরাণ কখনই আন্ধ্র, আভীর, গুপ্ত প্রভৃতি ভবিষ্য-রাজবংশের কাহিনীসম্বলিত বর্ত্তমান মহাপুরাণের সহিত অভিন্ন হইতে পারে না। যে হরিবংশে দীনার নামক রোমক মুদ্রার উল্লেখ আছে [১] উহা পাণিনির পূর্ব্বযুগের রচনা হইতে পারে না। বর্ত্তমান মহাভারতে কিন্তু আন্ধ্র, শক, আভীর, রোমক এমন কি হূণদিগেরও উল্লেখ দৃষ্ট হয়।

আন্ধ্রাঃ শকাঃ পুলিন্দাশ্চ যবনাশ্চ নরধিপাঃ।
কাম্বোজা বাহ্লিকাঃ শূরাস্তথাভীরাঃ নরোত্তমাঃ।
ন তদা ব্রাহ্মণঃ কশ্চিৎ স্বধর্ম্মমুপজীবতি। ৩।১৮৮।৩৫-৩৬

*   *   *   *

ঔষ্ণীকানন্তবাসাংশ্চ রোমকান্ পুরুষাদকান্। ২।৫১।১৭

*   *   *   *

চীনান্ শকান্ তথা চোড্রান্ বর্ব্বরান্ বনবাসিনঃ।
বার্ষ্ণেয়ান্ হারহূণাংশ্চ কৃষ্ণান্ হৈমবতাংস্তথা। ২।৫১।২৪

যবনেরা যে মহারাজ দত্তামিত্রের (Demetrios) নেতৃত্বে সিন্ধুসৌবীরে রাজ্য স্থাপন করিয়াছিল তাহার আভাস আদি-পর্ব্বে পাওয়া যায় :—

[১] প্রেষিতং দেবরাজেন দিব্যাভরণমম্বরম্।
আয়ুধানাং চ সর্ব্বেষাং ভাগা দীনারকা দশ॥
হরিবংশ—বিষ্ণুপর্ব্ব ৫৫, ৫০

ন শশাক বশেকর্ত্তুং যং পাণ্ডুরপি বীর্য্যবান্ ।
সোঽর্জ্জুনেন বশংনীতো রাজাসীদ্ যবনাধিপঃ ॥
অতীব বলসম্পন্নঃ সদা মানী কুরূন্ প্রতি ।
বিপুলো নাম সৌবীরঃ শস্তঃ পার্থেন ধীমতা ॥
দত্তামিত্র ইতি খ্যাতং সংগ্রামে কৃতনিশ্চয়ম্ ।
সুমিত্রং নাম সৌবীরমর্জ্জুনোঽ দময়চ্ছরৈঃ ॥

১।১৩৯।২১-২৩

এই দত্তামিত্রই ক্রমদীশ্বর কর্ত্তৃক উল্লিখিত দত্তামিত্রী নাম্নী সৌবীর-নগরীর প্রতিষ্ঠাতা। অর্জ্জুনের সহিত দত্তামিত্রের সংগ্রাম অনেকের নিকট বিস্ময়কর বলিয়া মনে হইবে, কিন্তু অনেক মহাকবিই এইরূপ দোষে (anachronism) দোষী।

মহাকবি কালিদাস কি দিগ্বিজয়ী রঘুর নিকট বঙ্খু বা বক্ষু (Oxus) তীরস্থিত হূণগণের পরাভবের উল্লেখ করেন নাই ?

মহাভারতের সমসাময়িক কালে হূণগণ যে চীনসীমান্তে আবদ্ধ ছিল না, পরন্তু পারসিকদিগের সংস্পর্শে আসিয়াছিল, নিম্নলিখিত শ্লোকে তাহা স্পষ্টই প্রতীয়মান হয় :—

যবনাশ্চীনকম্বোজা দারুণা ম্লেচ্ছজাতয়ঃ ।
সকৃদ্গ্রহাঃ কুলোত্থাশ্চ হূণাঃ পারসিকৈঃ সহ ।

৬।৯।৬৫-৬৬

হূণ-পারসিকসংযোগ আশ্বলায়ন বা পাণিনির পূর্ব্বে ঘটিয়াছিল ইহার কোন প্রমাণ নাই। ইতিহাস-পাঠে জানা যায় যে এই সংযোগের কাল খৃষ্টীয় ৫ম শতাব্দ। সুতরাং বর্ত্তমান মহাভারত যে প্রাক্-পাণিনীয় ভারত নহে এবং ইহার অনেক পরিবর্ত্তন ঘটিয়াছে ইহা অস্বীকার করিবার উপায় নাই। বস্তুতঃ মহাভারতে

উল্লিখিত আছে যে পূর্ব্বে উহা চতুর্ব্বিংশতি-সহস্র-শ্লোকাত্মক ছিল, অর্থাৎ উহার আয়তন বর্ত্তমান বিরাট-গ্রন্থের চতুর্থাংশের-ও কম ছিল—

চতুর্ব্বিংশতিসাহস্রীং চক্রে ভারত-সংহিতাম্।
উপাখ্যানৈর্বিনা তাবদ্ ভারতং প্রোচ্যতে বুধৈঃ। ১।১।১০২

চতুর্ব্বিংশতি সহস্র শ্লোকাত্মিকা সংহিতার পূর্ব্বে উহা অপেক্ষাও সংক্ষিপ্ত কোন ভারতকাব্য ছিল কিনা সে কথা বলা সহজ নহে। য়ুরোপীয় পণ্ডিতেরা মনে করেন যে তাহার পূর্ব্বে ৮৮০০ শ্লোকের একখানি মহাভারত ছিল, কিন্তু এই ধারণা নিতান্তই ভিত্তিহীন। ৮৮০০ এই সংখ্যা দ্বারা বর্ত্তমান গ্রন্থের কূটশ্লোকের সংখ্যা নির্দ্দেশ করা হইয়াছে।

গ্রন্থগ্রন্থিং তদা চক্রে মুনির্গূঢ়ং কুতূহলাৎ।
যস্মিন্ প্রতিজ্ঞয়া প্রাহ মুনির্দ্বৈপায়নস্ত্বিদম্।
অষ্টৌ শ্লোকসহস্রাণি অষ্টৌ শ্লোকশতানি চ।
অহং বেদ্মি শুকো বেত্তি সঞ্জয়ো বেত্তি বা ন বা।
তং শ্লোককূটমদ্যাপি গ্রথিতং সুদৃঢ়ং মুনে।
ভেত্তুং ন শক্যতেঽর্থস্য গূঢ়ত্বাৎ প্রশ্রিতস্য চ।
১।১।৮০-৮২

৮৮০০ শ্লোকের যে একখানি পূর্ণাবয়ব গ্রন্থ ছিল উহা উল্লিখিত উক্তি দ্বারা সমর্থিত হয় না; কিন্তু একথাও স্বীকার্য্য যে চতুর্ব্বিংশতি-সাহস্রী সংহিতা আদিম বৈয়াসকী সংহিতার সহিত অভিন্ন নাও হইতে পারে। যদি উহাদের অভিন্নতা মানিয়াও লওয়া যায় তাহা হইলেও বর্ত্তমান মহাভারতের ত্রি-চতুর্থাংশেরও অধিক পরবর্ত্তী কালে রচিত হইয়া উহার

অন্তর্নিবিষ্ট হইয়াছে সন্দেহ নাই। মহাভারতের অনেক অংশই যে প্রক্ষিপ্ত সে কথা বঙ্কিমচন্দ্র, রামকৃষ্ণ ভাণ্ডারকর, উদ্গীকর প্রভৃতি এদেশীয় মনীষিগণও স্বীকার করিয়াছেন। কিন্তু নূতন জিনিষ প্রক্ষিপ্ত করার সঙ্গে সঙ্গে আখ্যানভাগের আর কোন পরিবর্ত্তন কি হয় নাই? প্রাচীন আখ্যায়িকাগুলি কি সকলই অব্যাহত আছে? দ্রোণপর্ব্বের কতিপয় শ্লোক-পাঠে কিন্তু মনে হয় যে প্রাচীন মহাভারতে এমন অনেক আখ্যান ছিল অথবা মহাভারতকার এমন অনেক আখ্যানের বিষয় অবগত ছিলেন যাহার কেবল আভাস মাত্র প্রচলিত গ্রন্থে পাওয়া যায়, কিন্তু মূল আখ্যান বিলুপ্ত হইয়াছে। এই আখ্যানগুলি সর্ব্বপ্রাচীন বৈয়াসকী সংহিতার অন্তর্গত ছিল কিনা তাহা এখন বিচার্য্য নহে। কিন্তু প্রচলিত মহাভারত-সঙ্কলনের পূর্ব্বে যে এগুলির অস্তিত্ব ছিল তাহা অস্বীকার করিবার উপায় নাই।

দ্রোণপর্ব্বের ঘটোৎকচ-বধ পর্ব্বাধ্যায়ে লিখিত আছে যে কুরুক্ষেত্রের মহাযুদ্ধে মহাবীর কর্ণ ইন্দ্রদেব-প্রদত্ত একপুরুষ-ঘাতিনী শক্তি দ্বারা ভীমতনয় ঘটোৎকচের প্রাণ-সংহার করিলে পাণ্ডবগণকে শোককাতর দেখিয়া অসাধারণ ধীশক্তিসম্পন্ন বাসুদেব বলিয়াছিলেন, "যদি সূতপুত্র বাসবদত্ত শক্তি দ্বারা ঘটোৎকচকে নিহত না করিত তাহা হইলে আমাকেই বৃকোদর-পুত্রকে বধ করিতে হইত। আমি কেবল তোমাদের মঙ্গল-সাধনের নিমিত্তই পূর্ব্বে উহার জীবন নাশ করি নাই। এই নিশাচর ব্রাহ্মণবিদ্বেষী, যজ্ঞনাশক, ধর্ম্মলোপ্তা ও পাপাত্মা, এই নিমিত্ত কৌশলক্রমে নিপাতিত হইল।"

যদি হ্যেনং নাহনিষ্যৎ কর্ণঃ শক্ত্যা মহামৃধে
ময়া বধ্যোঽভবিষ্যৎ স ভৈমসেনির্ঘটোৎকচঃ।

ময়া ন নিহতঃ পূর্ব্বমেব যুষ্মৎ-প্রিয়েপ্সয়া,
এষ হি ব্রাহ্মণদ্বেষী যজ্ঞদ্বেষী চ রাক্ষসঃ
ধর্ম্মস্য লোপ্তা পাপাত্মা তস্মাদেব নিপাতিতঃ।

৭।১৭৯।২৫-২৭

ঘটোৎকচের ব্রাহ্মণবিদ্বেষ সম্বন্ধে কোন কাহিনী বর্ত্তমান মহাভারতে দেখিতে পাওয়া যায় না। কিন্তু কোন প্রাচীন ভারত-সংহিতায় উহা না থাকিলে বর্ত্তমান গ্রন্থে উপরি উদ্ধৃত শ্লোক-গুলি কি নিমিত্ত স্থান পাইল এবং উহার সার্থকতাই বা কি? শ্লোকগুলির পাঠে স্বতঃই মনে হয় যে উহাদের রচয়িতা হিড়িম্বা-তনয়ের ব্রাহ্মণবিদ্বেষ-মূলক কোন আখ্যানের বিষয় অবগত ছিলেন। যাঁহারা মধ্যমব্যায়োগ পাঠ করিয়াছেন তাঁহাদিগকে বলিয়া দিতে হইবে না যে এইরূপ একটি আখ্যান অবলম্বন করিয়া উক্ত নাট্যগ্রন্থ রচিত হইয়াছে। শকুন্তলোপাখ্যানের সহিত কালিদাস-প্রণীত অভিজ্ঞান-শকুন্তলের যে সম্বন্ধ, ঘটোৎকচের সেই বিলুপ্ত আখ্যানের সহিত মধ্যমব্যায়োগেরও ঠিক সেই সম্বন্ধ ছিল বলিয়া অনুমিত হয়। নাটককার অবশ্য নায়ক-চরিত্রের উৎকর্ষ-সাধনের জন্য অনেক বিষয়ে মৌলিকতা দেখাইয়া-ছেন। নাটকের দুষ্মন্তের শকুন্তলার প্রত্যাখ্যানের মূলে দুর্ব্বাসার অভিশাপ, নাটকের ঘটোৎকচের ব্রাহ্মণ-জন-বিত্রাসিত করার মূলে অনন্যসাধারণ মাতৃভক্তি। প্রিয়ংবদা, অনুসূয়া প্রভৃতির ন্যায় কেশবদাস, তপস্বী মধ্যম প্রভৃতি চরিত্র নাটক-কারের সৃষ্টি হওয়াও অসম্ভব নহে। কিন্তু মধ্যমব্যায়োগের মূল ঘটনা যে মহাভারতকারের অবিদিত ছিল না এবং খুব সম্ভব প্রাচীন কোন ভারত-সংহিতার অন্তর্নিবিষ্ট ছিল দ্রোণ-

পর্ব্ব হইতে উদ্ধৃত শ্লোকগুলি তাহার প্রকৃষ্ট প্রমাণ। সুতরাং ভারত-তত্ত্বানুসন্ধিৎসুদের পক্ষে গণপতি শাস্ত্রী-প্রকাশিত নাটক-গুলির আলোচনার যে যথেষ্ট প্রয়োজনীয়তা আছে তাহা অস্বীকার করিবার উপায় নাই।

CHAPTER XIV

বঙ্গ কোন্ দেশ ?

বঙ্গীয় সাহিত্য-সম্মিলনে পাঠের নিমিত্ত একটী ইতিহাস-বিষয়ক প্রবন্ধ লিখিতে বসিয়া মনে হইল বঙ্গের পুরাতত্ত্ব-সম্বন্ধে কিছু আলোচনা করিলে মন্দ হয় না। দ্রবিড়, কর্ণাট, মহারাষ্ট্র, রাজস্থান, পঞ্চনদ, পঞ্চাল, মগধ প্রভৃতি জনপদের প্রাচীন যুগের বিশদ বিবরণ দুষ্প্রাপ্য নহে, কিন্তু খাঁটী বাঙ্গালা দেশের প্রাচীন ইতিহাস আছে কি? সম্প্রতি গৌড়-বঙ্গের ঐতিহ্য-সম্বন্ধে কয়েকখানি গ্রন্থ প্রকাশিত হইয়াছে; কিন্তু উহাদের প্রথম অধ্যায়গুলিতে প্রধানতঃ অঙ্গ, মগধ, গন্ধার প্রভৃতি দেশেরই কীর্ত্তন করা হইয়াছে। অবশ্য গ্রন্থকারগণ বলেন যে প্রাচীন বঙ্গ অঙ্গ-মগধাদি রাষ্ট্রের সহিত দুশ্ছেছ্য সম্বন্ধে জড়িত। কিন্তু তাই বলিয়া মগধ-রাজবংশের ইতিহাস ও মৌর্য্য-রাষ্ট্রনীতির বিবরণ দ্বারা বঙ্গের ইতিহাসের কলেবর বৃদ্ধি করায় লাভ কি? বর্ত্তমানে এই প্রদেশ শ্বেত-মহারাষ্ট্রের অন্তর্ভূর্ত। সেই জন্য বাঙ্গালার ইতিহাস লিখিতে বসিয়া কি প্রত্যক্ শ্বেতদ্বীপের প্রাচীন রাজবংশ ও শাসনপ্রণালীর বিস্তৃত বিবরণ প্রদান করিতে হইবে? এবং উহাকেই "বঙ্গের ইতিহাস" এই নামে প্রখ্যাত করিতে হইবে?

প্রকৃত পক্ষে বঙ্গের পুরাতত্ত্ব আলোচনা করিতে হইলে বঙ্গ নামে কোন্ জনপদ বিশেষ ভাবে সূচিত হইত তাহা বুঝা কর্ত্তব্য। শক্তিসঙ্গমতন্ত্রে লিখিত আছে—

রত্নাকরং সমারভ্য ব্রহ্মপুত্রান্তগঃ শিবে
বঙ্গদেশো ময়া প্রোক্তঃ সর্ব্বসিদ্ধিপ্রদর্শকঃ। [১]

অর্থাৎ সমুদ্র হইতে ব্রহ্মপুত্র নদ পর্য্যন্ত বিস্তৃত ভূখণ্ডই বঙ্গ বলিয়া কথিত। এই শ্লোকে বঙ্গ ব্রহ্মপুত্রের পূর্ব্বভাগে কি পশ্চিমভাগে অবস্থিত তাহা ঠিক বুঝা গেল না। বাৎস্যায়নের কামসূত্রের টীকাকার যশোধর লিখিয়াছেন, "বঙ্গা লৌহিত্যাৎ পূর্ব্বেণ" [২] অর্থাৎ বঙ্গদেশবাসীরা লৌহিত্য বা ব্রহ্মপুত্র নদের পূর্ব্ব-তীরবাসী। বর্ত্তমান কালেও ব্রহ্মপুত্র-যমুনার পূর্ব্বকূলে অবস্থিত মৈমনসিংহ, ঢাকা, শ্রীহট্ট, ত্রিপুরা, চট্টগ্রাম প্রভৃতি অঞ্চলের অধিবাসিগণই বিশেষ ভাবে "বাঙ্গাল" বলিয়া অভিহিত হন। যশোধর খৃষ্টীয় ত্রয়োদশ শতাব্দীর লোক। [৩] তাঁহার পূর্ব্বে ব্রহ্মপুত্রের পশ্চিমেও যে বঙ্গদেশ বিস্তৃত ছিল সে বিষয়ে অনেক প্রমাণ পাওয়া যায়। মহাভারতে ভীমের দিগ্বিজয়-প্রসঙ্গে লিখিত আছে যে মধ্যম পাণ্ডব গিরিব্রজ, মোদাগিরি, পুণ্ড্র, কৌশিকী-কচ্ছ জয় করিয়া বঙ্গরাজকে আক্রমণ করিয়াছিলেন—"বঙ্গরাজ-মুপাদ্রবৎ।" পরে তাম্রলিপ্ত, কর্ব্বট, সুহ্ম এবং সাগর-তীরবর্ত্তী ম্লেচ্ছগণকে বশীভূত করিয়া লৌহিত্য-তীরে উপনীত হন। তিনি লৌহিত্য অতিক্রম করিয়া তাহার পূর্ব্বতীরবর্ত্তী ভূখণ্ডে গিয়াছিলেন ইহার কোনই প্রমাণ নাই। সুতরাং মহাভারত-রচনার যুগে বঙ্গ যে লৌহিত্যের পশ্চিমে বিস্তৃত ছিল ইহা সুনিশ্চিত

[১] শব্দ-কল্পদ্রুমে 'বঙ্গ' শব্দ দ্রষ্টব্য।

[২] Kāmasūtra, Published by the proprietor of the Chowkhamba Sanskrit Book Depot, p. 295

[৩] Keith, Sanskrit Literature, p. 469.

মহাকবি কালিদাসের রঘুবংশ-পাঠে মনে হয় যে তাঁহার সময়ে বঙ্গগণ "গঙ্গাস্রোতোঽন্তর" বর্ত্তী সমগ্র ভূখণ্ডই করায়ত্ব করিয়াছিল।

বঙ্গানুৎখায় তরসা নেতা নৌসাধনোদ্যতান্‌।
নিচখান জয়স্তম্ভান্‌ গঙ্গাস্রোতোঽন্তরেষু সঃ॥

বঙ্গগণ বশীভূত হইবার অব্যবহিত পরে মহাবীর রঘু গজময় সেতু দ্বারা কপিশা (মেদিনীপুরান্তর্গত কাঁসাই) নদী পার হইয়া উৎকল দেশে উপনীত হইয়াছিলেন। বঙ্গদেশ কি সত্য সত্যই কোন সময়ে কপিশা পর্য্যন্ত বিস্তৃত হইয়াছিল? জৈন উপাঙ্গ প্রজ্ঞাপনা-পাঠে কিন্তু তাহাই মনে হয়। প্রজ্ঞাপনাকার স্পষ্টতঃ "তামলিপ্তি" নগরীকে বঙ্গের অন্তর্ভূক্ত বলিয়া বর্ণনা করিয়াছেন।[১] এই স্থলে একটী সমস্যা স্বতঃ মনে উদিত হয়। দশকুমার-চরিত গ্রন্থে মহাকবি দণ্ডী "দামলিপ্ত" সুহ্মের অন্তর্ভূক্ত বলিয়া নির্দ্দেশ করিয়াছেন।[২] কালিদাসের যুগে বঙ্গ কপিশা পর্য্যন্ত বিস্তৃত ছিল এই কথা যদি সত্য হয়, তবে রঘুবংশকার সুহ্ম ও বঙ্গ পৃথক্‌ বলিয়া বর্ণন করিলেন কেন? ইহার উত্তর এই যে, দণ্ডীর সময়ের অবস্থা (খৃষ্টীয় সপ্তম কি অষ্টম শতাব্দী?[৩])

১ Ind. Ant., 1891, 375; JASB, 1908, 290.

২ ষষ্ঠোচ্ছ্বাস, মিত্রগুপ্ত-চরিতম্‌—JASB, 1908, 290n.
'দামলিপ্ত' ও 'তাম্রলিপ্ত' যে অভিন্ন তাহা হেমচন্দ্রের অভিধান-পাঠে জানা যায়। ত্রিকাণ্ড-শেষকার 'তমালিকা' বলিয়া আর একটী নামের উল্লেখ করিয়াছেন। মনোমোহন চক্রবর্ত্তী মহাশয়ের মতে উহাই তমলুক নামে পরিবর্ত্তিত হইয়াছে।

৩ Keith, Sanskrit Literature, p. 292; অবন্তিসুন্দরী-কথা

যাহাই হউক না কেন, প্রাচীনকালে সুহ্ম ও তাম্রলিপ্ত যে অভিন্ন ছিল না মহাভারতের দিগ্বিজয়-পর্ব্বই তাহার প্রকৃষ্ট প্রমাণ। মহাভারতকার তাম্রলিপ্তকে সুহ্ম এবং বঙ্গ উভয় হইতেই স্বতন্ত্র বলিয়া নির্দ্দেশ করিয়াছেন। মহাভারতের যুগে উহাই যে প্রকৃত অবস্থা ছিল তাহা অস্বীকার করিবার কারণ নাই। কিন্তু পরবর্ত্তী কালে তাম্রলিপ্ত কখনও বঙ্গ রাজ্যের এবং কখনও সুহ্ম রাজ্যের অন্তর্নিবিষ্ট হইত, প্রজ্ঞাপনা এবং দশকুমার গ্রন্থ ইহারই সাক্ষ্য প্রদান করে। এইরূপ ঘটনা ভারতের অন্যান্য প্রদেশেও দেখিতে পাওয়া যায়। অনেকেই উত্তরাপথের তক্ষশিলা নগরীর নাম শুনিয়াছেন। জাতকের যুগে ঐ নগরী গন্ধারের রাজধানী বলিয়া পরিচিত ছিল। যবন ভূতত্ত্ববিদ্ টলেমী উহাকে উরশা রাজ্যের অন্তর্ভূ্ত বলিয়া বর্ণনা করিয়াছেন। চীন পরিব্রাজক ফাহিয়ান ও হুয়েন-সাঙ্ কিন্তু তক্ষশিলাকে গন্ধার-বহির্ভূত একটী স্বতন্ত্র রাজ্য বলিয়া অভিহিত করিয়াছেন। সুদূর তামিল দেশের উরগপুরও কখনও চোল রাজ্য, কখনও পাণ্ড্য রাজ্যের অন্তর্ভূত হইত। কোটিবর্ষ দামোদরপুর লিপিতে পুণ্ড্রবর্দ্ধন-ভুক্তির এবং জৈন গ্রন্থ প্রজ্ঞাপনায় রাঢ়ের অন্তর্গত বলিয়া বর্ণিত হইয়াছে।

মহাভারত, রঘুবংশ, প্রজ্ঞাপনা এবং যশোধর-কৃত জয়মঙ্গলা প্রভৃতি গ্রন্থপাঠে স্পষ্টই মনে হয় যে "বঙ্গ" দুই অর্থে ব্যবহৃত হইত, একটী ব্যাপক, অপরটী সঙ্কীর্ণ। ব্যাপক অর্থে বঙ্গ বলিতে সময়ে সময়ে লৌহিত্যের পূর্ব্ব হইতে কপিশা পর্য্যন্ত বিস্তীর্ণ ভূখণ্ড বুঝাইত। সঙ্কীর্ণ বঙ্গ মগধ, মোদাগিরি, পুণ্ড্র, তাম্রলিপ্ত, কর্ব্বট, সুহ্ম এমন কি সাগরানূপ হইতেও পৃথক্ বলিয়া মহাভারতে নির্দ্দিষ্ট হইয়াছে। লক্ষ্মণ সেনের তাম্র-

শাসনের "বঙ্গে বিক্রমপুর ভাগে" এবং যশোধরের টীকায় "বঙ্গা লোহিত্যাৎ পূর্ব্বেণ" প্রভৃতি বাক্যে মনে হয় বিক্রমপুর ও তৎসন্নিহিত ব্রহ্মপুত্রের পূর্ব্বকূলস্থিত ভূখণ্ডই এই সঙ্কীর্ণ বঙ্গ। উত্তরকালে বঙ্গ যে সাগরানূপ পর্য্যন্ত বিস্তৃতি লাভ করিয়াছিল, শক্তিসঙ্গমতন্ত্রই তাহার প্রকৃষ্ট প্রমাণ। কিন্তু খৃষ্টীয় ষষ্ঠ শতাব্দীতে বরাহমিহির-কর্ত্তৃক রচিত বৃহৎসংহিতায় কূর্ম্মবিভাগ নামক চতুর্দ্দশ অধ্যায়েও সমুদ্রকূলবর্ত্তী "সমতট" ভূমি বঙ্গ হইতে পৃথক্ ভাবে উল্লিখিত হইয়াছে।

রাজেন্দ্রচোলদেবের তিরুমলয় লিপি ও চেদিপতি কর্ণদেবের গোহরবালিপিতে "বঙ্গাল" নামক দেশের উল্লেখ দৃষ্ট হয়। এই অভিনব নামটী কোন্ সময়ে সৃষ্ট হইয়াছে তাহা বলা দুরূহ। প্রাচীন সাহিত্য, শিলালেখ বা তাম্রপট্টে "বঙ্গ" নামেরই ব্যবহার ও প্রসিদ্ধি দেখা যায়। অদ্যাবধি আবিষ্কৃত প্রমাণ-দৃষ্টে মনে হয় যে, দক্ষিণাপথ ও তুরুস্ক দেশাগত ভূপতিগণই মধ্যযুগে "বঙ্গাল" বা বাঙ্গালা এই অভিনব নামের প্রয়োগ আরম্ভ করেন।[১] আইন-ই-আক্‌বরি-প্রণেতা আবুলফজল লিখিয়াছেন (২, ১২০) যে বাঙ্গালা প্রাচীন বঙ্গের নামান্তর মাত্র। পুরাকালে এতদ্ অঞ্চলের রাজন্যবর্গ সমগ্র প্রদেশে দশ গজ উর্দ্ধ ও বিংশ গজ আয়ত এক একটী আল্ অর্থাৎ মৃত্তিকাস্তূপ

[১] অধ্যাপক রমেশচন্দ্র মজুমদার মহাশয় কর্ণদেবের Goharwa Plateএর প্রতি আমার দৃষ্টি আকৃষ্ট করেন। উক্ত লিপিতে কর্ণদেবের বৃদ্ধপ্রপিতামহ লক্ষ্মণরাজ "বঙ্গাল ভঙ্গ নিপুণ" বলিয়া বিশেষিত হইয়াছেন। কিন্তু লক্ষ্মণরাজও উত্তরাপথের রাজা ছিলেন না।

প্রস্তুত করিয়া জলপ্লাবন নিবারণ করিতে চেষ্টা করিতেন। বঙ্গ+আল্ এই দুই শব্দের যোগে বঙ্গাল শব্দ নিষ্পন্ন হইয়াছে।

আশ্চর্য্যের বিষয় এই যে কলচুর্য্য-বংশোদ্ভব বিজ্জলের অবলূর লিপিতে বঙ্গ ও বঙ্গাল পৃথক্ বলিয়া নির্দ্দিষ্ট হইয়াছে।[১] অভিধান-চিন্তামণি-প্রণেতা জৈন হেমচন্দ্র লিখিয়াছেন—"বঙ্গাস্তু হরিকেলীয়া।" বঙ্গের সহিত অভিন্ন এই হরিকেল যে "বঙ্গাল" দেশ নহে, পরন্তু একটী স্বতন্ত্র ভূখণ্ড, ডাকার্ণব গ্রন্থে তাহার সুস্পষ্ট প্রমাণ পাওয়া যায়।[২] অতএব আবুলফজলের গ্রন্থে বঙ্গ ও বঙ্গাল এক দেশেরই ভিন্ন নাম বলিয়া লিখিত হইলেও পূর্ব্বে যে ঐ দুই নামে দুইটী পৃথক্ দেশ সূচিত হইত তাহা বলিলে বোধ হয় অন্যায় হয় না। বঙ্গ বা হরিকেল হইতে স্বতন্ত্র "বঙ্গাল" বলিতে কোন্ রাজ্য বুঝাইত এ বিষয়ে নিশ্চয় করিয়া বলা যায় না—বঙ্গাল যে দক্ষিণ ও উত্তর রাঢ়া হইতে বিভিন্ন এবং চন্দ্রোপাধিবিশিষ্ট গোবিন্দ নামক নরপতির অধীন ছিল, তিরুমলয় লিপিই তাহার প্রকৃষ্ট প্রমাণ। অধ্যাপক ব্লকম্যান লিখিয়াছেন যে, সুলতান সুজার রাজত্বকালে রঙ্গপুর ও ব্রহ্মপুত্রের মধ্যবর্ত্তী ভূখণ্ড "বঙ্গালভূম" বলিয়া প্রসিদ্ধ ছিল কিন্তু Blaev, Sausson Purchas-প্রমুখ লেখকগণের মানচিত্রে ও গ্রন্থে চট্টগ্রামের অভিমুখে অবস্থিত সাগরতীরবর্ত্তী ভূখণ্ডে Bengala নগরীর উল্লেখ দৃষ্ট হয়। ব্লকম্যান এই নগরীর অস্তিত্ব-সম্বন্ধে সন্দেহ

[১] *Ep. Ind.*, V. 257, *cf.* Elliot, iii. 295 (Afif).

[২] Majumdār, *Inscriptions of Bengal*, p. 61.

প্রকাশ করিয়াছেন, [১] কারণ ইবন্ বতুতা, সিজর ফ্রেডারিক, De Barros প্রভৃতি পর্য্যটক ও লেখকগণ ইহার কথা লিখিয়া যান নাই। ১৫৬১ খৃষ্টাব্দে অঙ্কিত Gastaldiর মানচিত্রে কিন্তু Bengalaর স্পষ্ট উল্লেখ দেখা যায়। সুতরাং সাগরানূপে সত্য সত্যই এই নামে একটী নগরী ছিল এইরূপ অনুমান নিতান্ত অসঙ্গত নহে। এই Bengala নগরীর চতুষ্পার্শ্বস্থিত রাজ্যই কি চন্দ্রোপাধিক নরপতি-শাসিত বঙ্গাল দেশ? শ্রীচন্দ্রের রামপাললিপি-পাঠে কিন্তু তাহাই মনে হয়। উক্ত লিপিতে শ্রীচন্দ্রের পিতা ত্রৈলোক্যচন্দ্রকে চন্দ্রদ্বীপের নৃপতি এবং "হরিকেল-রাজ-ককুদচ্ছত্রস্মিতানাং শ্রিয়ামাধারঃ" বলিয়া বর্ণন করা হইয়াছে। চন্দ্রদ্বীপ বলিতে সমুদ্র-তীরবর্ত্তী বর্ত্তমান বরিশাল এবং তৎসন্নিহিত ভূখণ্ড বুঝাইত। ইহাই শ্রীচন্দ্রের তাম্র-শাসনে চন্দ্রবংশীয় নরপতিগণের স্বরাজ্য বলিয়া নির্দ্দিষ্ট হইয়াছে। হরিকেল অর্থাৎ বঙ্গ ইহা হইতে স্বতন্ত্রভাবে উল্লিখিত হইয়াছে। চীন পরিব্রাজক ইৎসিং লিখিয়াছেন যে, হরিকেল ভারতের পূর্ব্ব সীমান্তে অবস্থিত। রাজশেখর-রচিত কর্পূরমঞ্জরী নামক গ্রন্থে পূর্ব্ব দিগঙ্গনা-গণের সম্পর্কে চম্পা, রাঢ়া, কামরূপ ও হরিকেলের উল্লেখ দৃষ্ট হয়। এই সকল উক্তির সহিত লক্ষ্মণ সেন দেবের তাম্রশাসন ও যশোধরের টীকা মিলাইয়া লইলে মনে হয় যে বিক্রমপুর ও লৌহিত্যের পূর্ব্বতীরস্থিত ভূখণ্ডই সপ্তম হইতে ত্রয়োদশ শতাব্দী পর্য্যন্ত "বঙ্গ" বা হরিকেল নামে প্রসিদ্ধ ছিল। সাগর-তীরবর্ত্তী "সাগরানূপ" বা "সমতট"

যে ইহার বহির্ভূত ছিল মহাভারত ও বৃহৎসংহিতা গ্রন্থে তাহার প্রমাণ পাওয়া যায়। "চন্দ্রদ্বীপ" ও "বঙ্গাল" এই উভয় দেশই বঙ্গ-বহির্ভূত সাগরানূপে অবস্থিত এবং চন্দ্রোপাধিক নৃপতি-শাসিত। ইহাদের ভৌগোলিক অবস্থান এবং চন্দ্রবংশের সহিত সংযোগ বিচার করিলে এই দুই দেশ যে অভিন্ন বা পরস্পর সংস্থষ্ট ইহা অনুমান করা বোধ হয় নিতান্ত অসঙ্গত হইবে না।

বিজ্জন বা বিজ্জলদেবের অবলূর-লিপি হইতে স্পষ্ট প্রতীয়মান হয় যে, শ্রীচন্দ্রদেবের বিক্রমপুর-বিজয় সত্ত্বেও খৃষ্টীয় দ্বাদশ শতাব্দীর শেষ পর্য্যন্ত বঙ্গ এবং বাঙ্গালা সম্পূর্ণভাবে একীকৃত হয় নাই। "রাঢ়" ও "বরেন্দ্র"ও স্বতন্ত্রতা রক্ষা করিতেছিল। ত্রয়োদশ শতাব্দীর মুসলমান লেখকগণ "বঙ্গ" শব্দ সঙ্কীর্ণ অর্থেই ব্যবহার করিয়াছেন। তবকাৎই-নাসিরি গ্রন্থে বঙ্গ স্পষ্টতঃ যাজনগর, কামরূপ ও ত্রিহুতের ন্যায় লক্ষ্মণাবতী হইতে বিভিন্ন বলিয়া বর্ণিত হইয়াছে। কিন্তু রাল (রাঢ়) ও বরিন্দ (বরেন্দ্র) লক্ষ্মণাবতীর অন্তর্গত ছিল। ব্লক্‌ম্যান দেখাইয়াছেন যে তুঘ্‌লুক্ শাহের রাজত্বকালেই (১৩২০ খৃঃ অব্দে) লক্ষ্মণাবতী, সপ্তগ্রাম ও সুবর্ণগ্রাম মিলিত হইয়া অখণ্ড বাঙ্গালা দেশ গঠিত হইয়াছে। জৈন প্রজ্ঞাপনায় এই মিলনের সূচনা দেখা যায়। বঙ্গপতি পালরাজগণ এবং প্রৌঢ়া রাঢ়ার অধীশ্বর সেন-নৃপতিবৃন্দ রাঢ়, গৌড়, বরেন্দ্র ও বঙ্গে একচ্ছত্র রাজ্য স্থাপন করিয়া ভাবী মিলনের পথ আরও সুগম করিয়া দিয়াছিলেন। মুসলমানগণ-কর্ত্তৃক লক্ষ্মণাবতী জয়ের ফলে এই মিলন সুদৃঢ় হইতে পারে নাই। কিন্তু তুঘ্‌লুক্ শাহ্ পুনরায় একচ্ছত্র রাজ্য প্রতিষ্ঠিত করিয়া স্থায়ী ঐক্য বিধান

করেন। পরবর্ত্তীকালে বঙ্গভঙ্গের সকল চেষ্টাই ব্যর্থ হইয়াছে।

সম্রাট্ আকবরের সময়ে সুবা বাঙ্গালা সুরমা-তীরবর্ত্তী শ্রীহট্ট হইতে কৌশিকী-ধৌত পূর্ণিয়া ও গঙ্গার দক্ষিণস্থিত Kankjol (কজঙ্গল) পর্য্যন্ত বিস্তৃত ছিল। মেদিনীপুর, হিজলী, চট্টগ্রাম এবং কোচবিহার তখনও এই প্রদেশের অন্তর্ভুক্ত হয় নাই। মেদিনীপুর ও হিজলী উড়িষ্যার এবং চট্টগ্রাম আরাকান রাজ্যের অন্তর্গত ছিল। কোচবিহার সীমান্তবর্ত্তী স্বাধীন রাজ্য বলিয়া পরিগণিত হইত। সম্রাট্ শাহ্জহান ও ঔরঙ্গজেবের রাজত্ব-কালে ক্রমে ক্রমে এই সকল ভূখণ্ড বাঙ্গালার অন্তর্নিবিষ্ট হয়। প্রত্যক্ শ্বেতদ্বীপের মহামাত্রগণ বাঙ্গালার উত্তর সীমা হিমবন্ত-প্রদেশ পর্য্যন্ত বিস্তৃত করিয়াছেন বটে, কিন্তু লৌহিত্য ও কৌশিকীর পূর্ব্বতীরস্থিত শ্রীহট্ট, পূর্ণিয়া প্রভৃতি কতকগুলি দেশ বাঙ্গালা হইতে বিচ্ছিন্ন করিয়া ইহাকে সুবা বাঙ্গালা অপেক্ষা হ্রস্বায়ত করিয়াছেন। [১]

১ বঙ্গীয় সাহিত্য-সম্মিলনের মাজু অধিবেশনের ইতিহাস-শাখায় পঠিত।

P. 17, line 18—After 'Krivis' add the name of the 'Sṛiñjayas' who constituted one section of the Pañchāla people [the other four being named 'Mudgala,' 'Bṛihadishu,' 'Yavînara,' and 'Kṛimilâśva, in the *Brahma Purāṇa* (XIII. 94-95). For the evidence of the Vedic texts on this point, see *Political History of Ancient India*, third edition, 47].

P. 62, margin—For 'Jambudvpia' read 'Jambudvîpa.'

P. 71, line 21—For 'Maru-parvata' read 'Meru-parvata.'

P. 84, line 11—For 'chatuḥ-saṁsthāna-saṁsthitam,' the *Brahmà Purāṇa* reads 'nava-saṁsthāna-saṁsthitam' (XXVII. 65). The former reading is to be preferred.

P. 89, line 6—The *Vāmana Purāṇa* twice (83.14 ; 90.42) mentions a Kaśeru-deśa in connection with Mount Pāriyātra.

P. 99, line 8—With the quadrangular mountains may be compared the *Kesara-parvatas* (*Brahma Purāṇa*, XVIII. 52) :—"Merośchaturdiśam ye tu proktāḥ Kesara-parvatāḥ." But the names of the Kesara-parvatas are not entirely identical with those of the "Quadrangular mountains" of Alberuni.

P. 111, line 9—Dikshitar (*Studies in Tamil Literature and History*, 13) distinguishes "Dakṣiṇa Madura" from the modern city of Madura.

P. 114 n 2—For '26' read '69.'

P. 136—

(1) Vaidyuta.—According to N. Dey "it is the Gurla range on the south of Lake Mānasa-Sarovara; the Saraju (Sarayu) is said to rise from this mountain" (*Brahmāṇḍa* P., Ch. LI).

(2) Kūṭa-śaila.—It may perhaps be connected with the Kuṭaka country which the *Bhāgavata Purāṇa* (V. 6. 9) associates with Koṅka(ṇa) and Veṅkaṭa in the Deccan. The *Devî-Bhāgavata* (VIII. 11) mentions Kūṭaka along with Ṛishabha, Kolla and Sahya, while the *Garuḍa Purāṇa* (II.7.68) associates "Kuṭalâchala" with the Kāverî.

(3) For 'Kristasmara' read 'Kṛitasmara.

(4) For 'Kora' read 'Chakora' (*cf.* Rapson *Andhra Coins*, xxxv).

(5) Añjana—N. Dey identifies it with the Suleiman Range on the authority of the *Varāha* Purāṇa, ch. 80. But it is difficult to find any evidence in support of this statement. The *Brahma Purāṇa* associates Añjana with the Gautamî, *i.e.*, the Godāvarî (Gautamyā dakshiṇe taṭe, girir Brahma-gireḥ pārśve Añjana nāma Nārada,

Ch. 84). The *Mārkaṇḍeya Purāṇa* (LVIII.11) places it in the east along with

Jambvākhyo Mānavāchalaḥ
Śurpa-Karṇo Vyāghramukhaḥ
Kharmakaḥ Karvaṭāśanaḥ

The *Mahābhārata* apparently places a 'Karvaṭa' in Bengal.

(6) Sūryādri and Kumudādri are placed in the Deccan. The former must, therefore, be carefully distinguished from the Himalayan peak called 'Saurya' (p.103 *ante*).

(7) Maṅgala-prastha.—The *Devî-Bhāgavata* (VIII.11.8) mentions it along with Malaya and other mountains of Southern India.

(8) Vāridhāra.—The *Devî-Bhāgavata* (VIII. 11. 9) associates it with the Vindhyas :—

Vāridhāraścha Vindhyaścha Śuktimān Ṛiksha-parvataḥ.

(9) Droṇa.—N. Dey identifies it with the Doonagiri mountain in Kumāun and refers to the *Devī Purāṇa*, Ch. 39. But verse 138 of that chapter connects Droṇa-parvata with Krauñcha-Dvîpa. The *Devī-Bhāgavata* (VIII.11.10) associates it with the Pāriyātra and Chitrakūṭa.

(10) Gokāmukha may be the same as Kokāmukha in the Himalayan region (Koketi prathitā loke Śiśirādri samāśritā, *Brahma* P., Ch. 219).

P. 176, line 25.—For "সর্ব্বনাথ" read "শর্ব্বনাথ".

Bibliographical Index

A

B

C

List of Periodicals, Miscellanies and Commemoration Volumes in which the Essays now collected, appeared for the first time :—

1. *The Calcutta Review* :—

(*a*) The Antiquity of the Rig-Veda (1924, Oct., 67f).

(*b*) Interrelation of the Two Epics of Ancient India (1922, March, 499f.).

(*c*) Aryan Occupation of India (1926, Oct., 123f).

2. *Journal of the Department of Letters*, Vol. XIX :—

(*d*) India in Purāṇic Cosmography (1929).

(*e*) The Mountain System of the Purāṇas (1929).

3. *Sir Asutosh Mookerjee Silver Jubilee Volumes*, Vol. III, Orientalia, Part 2, Calcutta (1921 and 1925) :—

(*f*) The Lakshmaṇa Sena Era.

4. *The Indian Antiquary* :—

(*g*) Epigraphic Notes (XLIX, 1920, 174-75).

5. *Journal of the Asiatic Society of Bengal* :—

(*h*) The Mahābhārata and the Besnagar Inscription of Heliodoros (1922, No. 19, p. 269f).

6. *The Indian Historical Quarterly* :—

(*i*) The Study of Ancient Indian Geography (June, 1928, 228f).

(*j*) A Note on the Vastrāpatha Māhātmya of the Skanda Purāṇa (March, 1929, 129f).

7. *Buddhistic Studies* (ed. Dr. B. C. Law) :—

(*k*) Buddhism in Western Asia (636f).

8. *Navya-Bhārata* :—

(*l*) মহাভারত ও বুদ্ধচরিত (৪১ বর্ষ, পৌষ, ১৩৩০, ৪৮৮-৯০পৃঃ).

9. *Mānasī O Marmavāṇī* :—

(*m*) বঙ্গ কোন দেশ ? (শ্রাবণ, ১৩৩৬, ৫৬৬-৬৯পৃঃ).

10. *Vichitrā* :—

(*n*) মহাভারত ও মধ্যমব্যায়োগ (অগ্রহায়ণ, ১৩৩৭, ৭৮৩-৮৬পৃঃ).

Geographical Index

General Index

H

I

J

K

L

M

N

P

BY THE SAME AUTHOR

(OPINIONS AND REVIEWS)

I. Political History of Ancient India

From the Accession of Parikshit to the Extinction of the Gupta Dynasty

First Edition, 1923.

Royal 8vo, 350 pp. Price Rs. 4.

Published by the Calcutta University.

DR. L. D. BARNETT, LONDON.—" The author treats his materials with a certain degree of originality, but at the same time he preserves throughout a well-balanced judgment and never sacrifices critical caution to the passion for novel theories......This interesting book...... shews judgment, ingenuity, and learning. And not the least of the author's merits is that he can write plain English " (the *Calcutta Review*, Feb., 1924).

PROFESSOR HULTZSCH, HALLE, GERMANY.—" Your valuable work......is the outcome of extensive researches and throws much light on the darkest and most debated periods of Indian history. You have succeeded in building up an intelligible account from the stray and imperfect materials which are available to the historian of those times."

PROFESSOR JOLLY, WÜRZBURG, GERMANY.—" Many thanks for your splendid volume.........What an enormous mass of evidence has been collected and discussed in this work, an important feature of which is the quotation of the original texts along with their translation which makes it easy to control the conclusions arrived at. The ancient geography, not less than the ancient history of India, has been greatly furthered by your researches and much new light has been thrown on some of the most vexed problems of Indian Archaeology and Chronology. The indices are very copious and the study of your work is greatly facilitated by them."

PROFESSOR PELLIOT, PARIS.—" Le nom de l'auteur est garant du serieux du travail."

PROFESSOR JARL CHARPENTIER, UPSALA. SWEDEN.—" Professor Ray Chaudhuri belongs to a set of young Hindu scholars who, combining the traditional education of a Pandit with a thorough training in English, German or French Universities, have lately been carrying on deep and fruitful researches in the various domains of Indian lore......Even the student, who on essential points does differ widely from the opinions expressed by Professor Ray Chaudhuri, must willingly recognize his high merits as a scholar."

PROFESSOR A. SCHEPOTIEFF, UFA, RUSSIA.—" For our study of the history of the Ancient Age your Political History of Ancient India is of very great importance" (trans. from original).

Second edition, 1927.
Royal 8vo, pp. xix, 416.

C. E. A. W. OLDHAM (*JRAS*, 1928, pp. 689-692).—This is a revised and considerably enlarged edition of Professor Ray Chaudhuri's work, first published in 1923. Part I deals with the period from Parikṣit to Bimbisāra. The author seeks to show, as he tells us in his preface, " that chronological relation of the national transactions before 600 B.C. is not impossible." He has laid under contribution the usual authorities—the Vedic, Puranic, Buddhist, and Jaina texts—though he does not appear to place much reliance upon the last named (*cf.* pp. 6 and 72). A vast mass of records has been collated, and the evidence marshalled in a very concise and able, and in some respects original, manner. The apposite quotations from the original texts are useful. Professor Ray Chaudhuri regards Parikṣit I and Parikṣit II, as they are named by the late Mr. Pargiter in his *Ancient Indian Historical Tradition*, as being probably one and the same king, and as identifiable with the Vedic Parikṣit. By " the great Janaka " he refers to the Janaka of the later Vedic texts, whose court is said to have been thronged with Brāhmaṇas, and not to the traditional first king Janaka, the eponymous founder of the Janakavaṁśa, or to Janaka Sīradhvaja, the reputed father of Sītā. Synchronizing Guṇākhya Sāṅkhāyana with Āśvalāyana and the Buddha, he inclines, it seems, to place Parikṣit in the ninth, and the " great Janaka " in the seventh century B.C. though he wisely avoids coming to any positive conclusion as to these debatable dates, and points out that if the evidence of the Purāṇas were accepted we would have to place them some five centuries earlier. If it could be established that Parikṣit came into power at the beginning of the ninth century, or the end of the tenth, this would help to corroborate the approximate chronology suggested by Mr. Pargiter, having regard also to the synchronism between Senapati Bārhadratha and Adhisīmakṛṣṇa. But until more convincing evidence is discovered, most scholars will probably agree in the verdict of Vincent Smith, that nothing approaching exact chronology is yet available for periods anterior to about 650 B.C.

Much of the matter in Part II will perhaps be familiar to students of Indian history ; but it has been arranged in a fresh and scholarly manner, while several important suggestions have been made on different questions. One or two of these may be cited as examples. On pp. 72-3 reasons are set forth for accepting the Ceylon tradition that Siśunāga was later than Bimbisāra. The view recorded by Mahāmahopādhyāya H. P. Śāstrī that the ultimate dismemberment of the Mauryan empire was due to a reaction promoted by the Brāhmaṇas, is vigorously controverted. Whatever other causes may have operated and Professor Ray Chaudhuri undoubtedly lays his finger on more than one such. Brahmanical influences cannot be ignored. The arguments used for holding that Demetrius,[1] rather than Menander, was the Yavana invader of the Madhyadeśa in the time of Pushyamitra. and that Simuka, the founder of the Sātavāhana dynasty, must be placed in the first century B.C., deserve careful consideration.

Since Hoernle made his well-known suggestion as to the identity of Devagupta, mentioned in two inscriptions of Harṣavardhana, several writers have attempted to frame the history of the later Guptas of Eastern Mālava and Bihār and the Maukharis of Kanauj. The period presents many difficulties. which are not likely to be solved until some further evidence reveals itself. Having regard to the conditions of the times and the bitter enmity of the Maukharis, who were then very powerful, it seems unlikely that the Susthitavarman mentioned in the Aphsaḍ inscription of Ādityasena as having been defeated by Mahāsenagupta of E. Mālava, could have been the king of Kāmarūpa, as the author states. Fleet's suggestion that he was the Maukhari king of that name,[2] whom we know to have been contemporaneous with Mahāsenagupta, seems more probable.

Not the least valuable part of the contents of this volume are the numerous comments on the geographical

1 For the latest reading of the Hāthigumphā inscription reference to the Yavana king, see *JBORS*, XIII, 228.

2 No Maukhari king of that name is known [H.C.R.C.].

information supplied in the records quoted ; and it is a matter of regret that of the five maps entered in the table of contents (p. xvi), only one, *viz.*, that of " Bhāratavarsha " appears in the volume before us. As regards this map we are not told what specific period, if any, it refers to. In any case, the positions assigned to the Niṣādas, S. Kosala, Kāmboja, and the Ṛikṣa mountains seem to call for some explanation. On the other hand, the geographical information given in the text is extensive, and often suggestive, and it indicates that much attention has been devoted to this important auxiliary to ancient Indian historical research. The indexes, both bibliographical and general, have been very well prepared.

PROFESSOR A. BERRIEDALE KEITH, EDINBURGH.—I have to express my appreciation of the courtesy of the University of Calcutta in forwarding to me at the request of the author a copy of Dr. H. C. Ray Chaudhuri's Political History of Ancient India, which I observe, has reached a second edition.

I have now read through the work and find it to contain much that is valuable. The author has arrived at clearly cut opinions on many of the chief difficulties in the history of early India ; he has formulated them effectively, and as a result, even when they do not commend themselves as final solutions, they will serve to promote the discussion and to facilitate further fruitful research. He observes a due sense of proportion and is well read in the literature. The work accordingly may justly be deemed a most valuable contribution to the subject-matter of which it treats.

PROFESSOR WILH GEIGER, MUNCHEN-NEUBIBERG, GERMANY,—Tell my best thanks, please, to Mr. H. C. Ray Chaudhuri for kindly presenting me with his splendid work on Political History of Ancient India from the time of Parikṣit down to the extinction of the Gupta dynasty, and excuse my delay in writing you. But I was absent from home, and it is only a short time ago that I returned from our hills where I have spent some holiday weeks. I highly appreciate Mr. Ray Chaudhuri's work as a most happy combination of sound scientific method and enormous knowledge of both Brahmanical and non-Brahmanical literature. The work is written in lucid style inspite of its intricate subject and affords a mass of valuable evidence, throwing much light on the whole period of Indian History dealt with in it. I see with special pleasure and satisfaction that we now are enabled by the author's penetrating researches to start in Indian chronology from the 9th instead of the 6th or 5th century B.C.

K. P. Jayaswal, Patna.—I am very thankful to you for your valuable book. I am glad that you devote your attention to Hindu geography as well.

Professor Jackson, Columbia University, New York. —I can see the scholarly research which you have put into the volume, and am glad to have such a work for future reference in my historical studies.

Professor Louis de la Valle'e Poussin, Brussels, Belgium.—I believe that the book is well designed and has the twofold merit of collecting a vast amount (and in some chapters, an exhaustive one) of references, and of giving a clear and reasonable *exposé* of the main line of this history. I agree with the author on several controverted points of chronology.

Mrs. C. A. F. Rhys Davids (BSOSL, Vol. IV, pp. 857 ff).—Dr. Chaudhuri has made debtors of us all.

II. Political History of India

From the Accession of Parikshit to the Coronation of Bimbisāra.

Reprint from the Journal of the Department of Letters, Vol. IX, Royal 8vo, 96 pp. :—

PROFESSOR E. WASHBURN HOPKINS.—" It is a fine augury for Indian scholarship when native scholars of the first rank take seriously in hand the great problem of untangling the web of Indian history. To this work your book is a valuable contribution."

PROFESSOR H. JACOBI, BONN.—" Very suggestive and contains some important details."

PROFESSOR F. OTTO SCHRADER.—"I have read the book with increasing interest and do not hesitate to say that it contains a great many details which will be found useful by later historians. The portion I enjoyed most is that on the sixteen Mahājanapadas."

PROFESSOR A. BERRIEDALE KEITH.—" Full of useful information."

PROFESSOR L. D. BARNETT, BRITISH MUSEUM.—" Presents the facts very well. It will be very useful to students."

PROFESSOR E. J. RAPSON, CAMBRIDGE.—" I write to thank you for your kindness in sending me copies of your interesting papers."

S. M. EDWARDES (Indian Antiquary, January, 1924).—One cannot wholly reject as imaginary the traditional figures mentioned in ancient history, particularly when their existence, circumstances and achievements are so carefully co-ordinated and illustrated by quotation as they are is this modest, but withal interesting, volume.

W. CHARLES DE SILVA, COLOMBO.— 'I have the greatest pleasure to express my high appreciation of your very valuable and learned article."

III. The Early History of the Vaishnava Sect

Demy 8vo, 146 pp. Price Rs. 2-13
Published by the Calcutta University.

PROFESSOR E. WASHBURN HOPKINS, YALE UNIVERSITY, AMERICA.—" Your book has given me great satisfaction.........I am particularly pleased to see an incisive study of this kind in the realm of religious history......... Believe me, in the hope of further contributions of this character from your able pen......"

PROFESSOR A. BERRIEDALE KEITH, EDINBURGH UNIVERSITY.—" While I do not concur in your view as to the original character of Kṛṣṇa, I recognise the care with which you have investigated the issue, and value highly the elaborate collation of the evidence which your work contains, and which will render it of much service to all students of this, doubtless insoluble, problem. The stress laid on the epigraphic evidence and the full use made of it is of special value, while in many details your opinions are of interest and value, as in the case of the date of Pāṇini........."

SIR GEORGE GRIERSON.—" Very interesting and informing.........The book is full of matter which is of great importance for the history of religion in India and will form a valued addition to my collection of books on the subject........."

F. E. PARGITER, OXFORD.—"I agree with you in discarding various theories, but I don't think that Kṛṣṇa Devakiputra is the famous Kṛṣṇa, and it seems to me your exposition can stand just as well without the identification as with it. Your book will help to elucidate the whole matter, but are you sure that the cult does not owe something to Christianity?"

PROFESSOR F. OTTO SCHRADER, KIEL, GERMANY.—"I perfectly agree with your opinion that the Chāndogya passage on Kṛṣṇa Devakiputra and his teaching is to be considered as the first historical record of Bhagavatism. There were, of course, many Kṛṣṇas, but to conjecture that more than one was also a Devakiputra, is to my mind an unscientific boldness which is the less justifiable as the teachings mentioned in that passage, as you show, perfectly agree with those, *e.g.*, of the Bhagavad-gitā and the Ṛk quoted with the famous तद्विष्णो परमं पदं।........."

PROFESSOR GARBE, TÜBINGEN, GERMANY.—"I have read your book with the greatest interest and perfectly agree with you in the main points, as to the personality of Kṛṣṇa and the development of Bhāgavatism.........You have brought together much important material and elucidated the dark early history of Bhāgavatism as far as possible."

THE TIMES LITERARY SUPPLEMENT, MAY 12, 1921.—"The lectures of Mr. Hemchandra Ray Chaudhuri on the early history of the Vaishṇava Sect read almost as would a Bampton lecture on the "Historical Christ" to a Christian audience. They are an attempt to disentangle the authentic figure of Krishna from the mass of Puranic legend and gross tradition, from the wild conjectures and mistaken, if reasoned, theories which surround his name. The worship of Krishna is not a superstitious idolatry ; it is the expression of the Bhakti, the devotional faith of an intellectual people, and many missionaries, ill-equipped for dealing with a dimly understood creed would do well to study this little volume......"

JOURNAL ASIATIQUE, JANUARY-MARCH, 1923, PARIS.—"Dans le domaine historique, signalons un travail plein de merite de M. Hemchandra Ray Chaudhuri : *Materials for the study of the Early History of the Vaishnava Sect.*" (Dr. Jules Bloch of Paris.)

DR. JULES BLOCH, PARIS.—" My Guru, Sylvain Lévi, who has come back from his travels, told me also of his esteem for that book."

JOURNAL OF THE ROYAL ASIATIC SOCIETY OF GREAT BRITAIN.—"The scope of this small book is rightly expressed in its title. The author who is Lecturer in History in the Calcutta University, has collected and discussed statements, references, and allusions from the early literature to throw light on the position and life of Kṛṣṇa and the growth of Bhāgavatism. He deals with the various theories that have been put forward, and with good reasons discredits the views that Kṛṣṇa Vāsudeva was a solar deity or a tribal god or a vegetation deity. He is right in treating Kṛṣṇa Vāsudeva as one person, the Vṛṣṇi chief, but he unnecessarily identifies him with Kṛṣṇa Devakīputra, the scholar mentioned in the Chāndogya Upanishad ......" (F. E. Pargiter).

THE BOMBAY CHRONICLE, JUNE 19, 1921.—" In this small book of a hundred and seventeen pages, Mr. Hemchandra Ray Chaudhuri of the Calcutta University has collected much valuable material from which he has succeeded in tracing the origin and growth of the Vaishnava creed. The Historicity of Srikrishna—or as the author calls him, Krishna Vāsudeva—is also handled with remarkable clearness.........."

IV. The Antiquity of the Rig Veda

PROFESSOR SCHRADER, KIEL, GERMANY.—This is a sober and useful little piece of research work with which, on the whole, I fully agree. If we follow Jacobi and Tilak we create a gap (which we cannot bridge over) between the Mantras and the Brāhmaṇas, for the latter are certainly not far removed from early Buddhism. On the other hand, if Hertel were right, the Rig Veda would immediately precede Buddhism, and there would be no room at all for Brāhmaṇas and Upaniṣads.

V. The Mahabharata and the Besnagar Inscription of Heliodoros

JASB, 1922, No. 19.

PROFESSOR H. JACOBI.—"The verification of the Bhāgavata credo in the Besnagar inscription is a find on which you may be congratulated."

PROFESSOR E. WASHBURN HOPKINS.—"It is certainly a remarkable resemblance which you have established and I should be inclined to agree with your conclusion."

PROFESSOR JARL CHARPENTIER.—"The identification of some words in this very important document with a passage in the Mahābhārata seems to be a most happy find."

VI. Interrelation of the Two Epics of Ancient India

PROFESSOR SCHRADER, KIEL, GERMANY.—Very many thanks for your important paper on the inter relation of the two epics. The opinion held by Macdonell, Winternitz, and others, *viz.*, that the heroes of the Mahābhārata are unknown to the Rāmāyaṇa, seems, indeed, to be untenable.......Again, I find it difficult, as you do, to distinguish between a Pāṇḍava story and a Kuru-Bhārata Epic.

DR. L. D. BARNETT, LONDON.—I think you have made out a good case.

VII. The Aryan Occupation of India, Calcutta Review, 1926, Oct.

India in Purāṇic Cosmography.
The Mountain System of the Puranas. } Journal of the Department of Letters, XIX.

A Note on the Vastrāpatha Māhātmya of the Skanda-purāṇa—Indian Historical Quarterly, March, 1929.

PROF. RAPSON.—I have read them with much interest and shall carefully preserve them for future reference.

DR. BARNETT.—They are very interesting and critically sound.

DR. KEITH.—They are all very interesting, and I am glad to note the very useful information elicited as to Bhoja.

VIII. The Lakshmana Sena Era

Reprint from Sir Asutosh Mookerjee Silver Jubilee Volumes, Vol. III, Orientalia, Part 2, Calcutta.—Published by the Calcutta University and printed at the Baptist Mission Press, 1921 and 1925.

PROFESSOR DR. STEN KONOW, KRISTIANIA, NORWAY.—"Many thanks for the reprints which you have been good enough to send me. I have read them with great pleasure. They are written in a thoroughly scholarlike way, and more especially it seems to me that your paper about the Lakṣmaṇa Sena era deserves very careful attention."